Write to the Core

Write to the Core

Inspiring Young Writers through Mindfulness and Poetry

Laura Bean

ROWMAN & LITTLEFIELD
Lanham • Boulder • New York • London

Published by Rowman & Littlefield
An imprint of The Rowman & Littlefield Publishing Group, Inc.
4501 Forbes Boulevard, Suite 200, Lanham, Maryland 20706
www.rowman.com

86-90 Paul Street, London EC2A 4NE

Illustrations courtesy of Leslie Shelton.

British Library Cataloguing in Publication Information Available

Library of Congress Cataloging-in-Publication Data

Names: Bean, Laura, 1966– author.
Title: Write to the core : inspiring young writers through mindfulness and poetry / Laura Bean.
Description: Lanham : Rowman & Littlefield Publishers, [2023] | Includes bibliographical references.
Identifiers: LCCN 2022045247 (print) | LCCN 2022045248 (ebook) | ISBN 9781475866247 (cloth) | ISBN 9781475866254 (paperback) | ISBN 9781475866261 (ebook)
Subjects: LCSH: Affective education. | English language—Composition and exercises—Study and teaching (Middle school) | English language—Composition and exercises—Study and teaching (Secondary) | Mindfulness (Psychology) | Poetry—Study and teaching (Middle school) | Poetry—Study and teaching (Secondary) | Motivation in education.
Classification: LCC LB1072 .B428 2023 (print) | LCC LB1072 (ebook) | DDC 370.15/34—dc23/eng/20221129
LC record available at https://lccn.loc.gov/2022045247
LC ebook record available at https://lccn.loc.gov/2022045248

∞™ The paper used in this publication meets the minimum requirements of American National Standard for Information Sciences—Permanence of Paper for Printed Library Materials, ANSI/NISO Z39.48-1992.

Dedication

This book is dedicated to my parents,
for giving me the breath of life,
to my teachers, for reminding me who I am,
and to young people everywhere.

Poetry is the smallest way—it is a small, small way, but it is a way indeed—that the individual body can express its own personhood and value in the face of faceless systems. —Kazin Ali

Permissions

David Whyte, "Everything Is Waiting for You," © *Many Rivers Press*, Langley, Washington, USA.

Pablo Neruda, "A callarse" (Keeping Quiet), *Extravagaria*, © Pablo Neruda, 1958 and Fundacion Pablo Neruda.

"Keeping Quiet," from *Extravagaria* by Pablo Neruda, translated by Alastair Reid. Translation copyright ©1974 by Allister Reid. Reprinted by permission of Farrar, Straus, and Giroux. All Rights Reserved.

Coleman Barks, translator. *The Essential Rumi*, by Jalal al-Din Rumi, HarperCollins, 1995.

"Love after Love" from Sea Grapes by Derek Walcott, © 1976 by Derek Walcott, Reprinted by permission of Farrar, Straus, and Giroux. All Rights Reserved.

From *Writing Down the Bones: Freeing the Writer Within*, by Natalie Goldberg, © 1986 by Natalie Goldberg. Reprinted by arrangement with The Permissions Company, LLC, on behalf of Shambhala Publications Inc., www.shambhala.com.

"The Summer Day" by Mary Oliver, Reprinted by the permission of The Charlotte Sheedy Literary Agency as agent for the author. Copyright © NW Orchard LLC 1990 with permission of Bill Reichblum.

"So Much Happiness" and "Kindness" from *Words Under the Words: Selected Poems* by Naomi Shihab Nye, copyright © 1995. Used with the permission of Far Corner Books.

Contents

Foreword, *Dr. Amy Saltzman* ... xi

Acknowledgments ... xv

Introduction ... xvii

Chapter 1
Becoming a Mindful Educator ... 1

Chapter 2
Building Resiliency ... 5

Chapter 3
Anatomy of a Mindful Writing Lesson ... 7

Lesson 1
Creating a Practice Community: "Give a Little Love" by Charlie Fink ... 11

Lesson 2
The Gift of Attention: "The Summer Day" by Mary Oliver ... 29

Lesson 3
Belonging to the Natural World: Excerpt, "Song of Myself," Section 2,
by Walt Whitman ... 47

Lesson 4
Why Practice Mindfulness? "Keeping Quiet" by Pablo Neruda ... 63

Lesson 5
Self-Compassion: "Kindness" by Naomi Shihab Nye ... 83

Lesson 6
Welcoming Difficult Emotions: "The Guest House" by Jalal al-Din Rumi 101

Lesson 7
Acceptance: "So Much Happiness" by Naomi Shihab Nye 119

Lesson 8
Befriending Oneself: "Love After Love" by Derek Walcott 137

Lesson 9
Noticing Habits: "Autobiography in Five Short Chapters"
by Portia Nelson 153

Lesson 10
Empathy and Compassion: "Saint Francis and the Sow"
by Galway Kinnell 175

Lesson 11
Forgiveness: "Revenge" by Taha Muhammad Ali 193

Lesson 12
Joy: "Everything Is Waiting for You" by David Whyte 215

Culminating Activities 235

Appendix 239

About the Author 245

Foreword

Dear passionate, committed, overworked, underappreciated English Language Arts, English Language Development, and Special Education teachers and advisors,

This book is a gift. Actually, it contains several gifts—an engaging reading and writing curriculum, a supportive social-emotional learning curriculum, and a guide for creating a community of meaningful connection and kindness in your classroom. The book's most precious gift is a deep, compassionate process to help you and your students discover and express your own hearts.

I am a physician, author, mindfulness facilitator, and the co-founder and director of the Association of Mindfulness in Education. I also chaired the UC San Diego Bridging Hearts and Minds of Youth conference for six years. Over the last two decades, I have shared my own mindfulness curricula with youth in woefully under-resourced schools, extremely affluent independent schools, and everywhere in between. Dozens of teachers, counselors, and youth group facilitators have requested my support in tailoring mindfulness curricula for their unique communities. And I have been asked to review and endorse scores of other curricula.

I am discerning—some might even say picky—and the book you hold in your hands is one of the very best.

I first met Laura when she participated in a ten-week online training for teachers interested in offering my Still Quiet Place Curriculum to youth. During the training, Laura shared about her experience teaching English as a Second Language in Japan for ten years. During that decade, she deepened her mindfulness practice, working closely with a master teacher and spending several weeks each year participating in silent meditation retreats. She also served as developmental editor for her teacher's first book.

After participating in my online training, Laura chose to shadow me during an eight-week, in-person course for tweens. Her devoted mindfulness practice and passion for offering essential life skills to young people were evident in her caring interactions with the participants. During the course, she also began weaving her enthusiasm for creative writing into my curriculum. By pairing poems and writing prompts with each of the lessons, she created an exquisite, potent new "language arts" curriculum.

I recognized the enormous potential for this curriculum to transform secondary classrooms and suggested she write this book, which is much more than a "language arts" curriculum.

It has been a privilege and a joy to support Laura in bringing this book to life. She knows firsthand the day-to-day realities of teaching in twenty-first-century classrooms: the emphasis on testing and teaching to Standards, the lack of support and resources, and the many struggles that teachers and students face in their lives outside the classroom. Much of this curriculum was developed while Laura was teaching at a large middle school in a community where violence is commonplace.

After her class read the poem "Kindness" by Naomi Shihab Nye, in a lesson centered around the theme of self-compassion, one twelve-year-old girl wrote the following story; it exemplifies the trauma far too many of our students carry with them into classrooms every day.

Tenth Street Tragedy

> I think it was Thanksgiving. My cousin and his friend Arturo were walking to the corner store to buy sodas and soups. All of the sudden someone started shooting at them. My cousin got shot on the leg and he couldn't walk, but they kept shooting. He was screaming and Arturo was running to help him. They shot Arturo three times and the last bullet hit his heart.
>
> We heard the gunshots from my house, so my family and I went running to go see who got shot. When we got there, the car drove off. My aunt saw that it was her son lying on the sidewalk and she hugged him and started to cry. We called the ambulance and they came quick. My cousin was crying and saying, "This is my fault!" He got close to his friend and said, "I love you and I'll take care of you." Arturo said, "Take care. I love you too," and then he closed his eyes.
>
> —Veronica T., age 12

Reading personal stories from your students will help you understand the pain they carry just below the surface. It will evoke your natural empathy and compassion for behaviors that you may have initially found confusing, difficult, or even disrespectful. Trauma specialists encourage us to remain calm and curious about the young people we serve, and to ask, "What happened to you?" rather than "What's wrong with you?"

Gun violence is a devastating reality many of our students face, and none are able to escape the perils of modern society. They experience bullying in school and online. Social media promotes the message that they're not good enough. Broader issues like climate change, racism, and social polarization loom large.

Rooted in mindfulness and self-compassion practices, this curriculum offers an ideal method for students to share their worries and fears, while simultaneously improving their reading and writing skills. With these easy-to-implement lessons and your natural compassion as your guides, you can encourage your students to explore their feelings and share some of the stories that color their perceptions, attitudes, willingness, and ability to engage in your classroom.

The curriculum is research based. Mindfulness and compassion practices have been scientifically proven to decrease anxiety, depression, and self-harming behaviors, while enhancing resilience and a sense of meaning and purpose. Each lesson includes a brief section on current related research in neuroscience and positive psychology.

Laura's decades of teaching English and practicing mindfulness are palpable on every page. She gently introduces a means to work with intense emotions like self-loathing, fear, and anger, and discusses sensitive topics like loss and forgiveness. If I am in a setting where I have time to share only one mindfulness practice with young people, I offer a "Befriending Feelings" practice. In chapter 9, "Welcoming Difficult Emotions," Laura provides a powerful iteration on this practice, using Rumi's poem "The Guest House" as a foundation. The result is that students have the opportunity to explore tender emotional territory, while practicing their writing skills, as exemplified in the following collaborative poem by middle schoolers:

> This being human is a city—
> every morning, traffic jams, donuts, the homeless,
> fear, worry, depression, happiness, delight.
>
> Welcome and entertain them all!
> Even if they're drug dealers
> who have guns and smoke weed,
> still offer them holy water.
>
> Be grateful to whoever comes
> because they are still a part of the city.

In closing, it is my sincere belief that this curriculum will benefit you and your students. It will literally breathe life into your teaching, enhancing your students' reading comprehension, creative thinking, and self-expression. More importantly, it will offer you and your students opportunities to connect to your most essential selves, cultivate much-needed social-emotional skills, and offer kindness to yourselves, each other, and the broader community. This book makes it simple and easy to bring your compassionate heart to the core curriculum, and it invites your students to do the same. It is an ideal antidote to the intense stresses and numbing challenges of modern education.

Amy Saltzman, MD
director of the Association for Mindfulness in Education
Author of *A Still Quiet Place: A Mindfulness Program for Teaching Children and Adolescents to Ease Stress and Difficult Emotions*
Santa Barbara, 2021

Acknowledgments

I owe a deep debt of gratitude to many—to my meditation teachers, for encouraging me to pause and look inward; to my mentor, Dr. Amy Saltzman, for first suggesting that I write this book and guiding me through to its completion; and to early supporters—Susan Gause, Tom Nazario, and Jennifer Zahgkuni from The Forgotten International.

I'd also like to acknowledge the poets for their inspiration and dedication to their craft. A special note of gratitude goes to Naomi Shihab Nye for her enthusiastic support and generosity. Many thanks to Leslie Shelton for the beautiful illustrations, to Tim Iverson for insightful editing and encouragement, and to Robert Pimm for his advocacy and sense of humor.

Lastly, I'd like to say thank you to dear friends who reviewed lessons, offered helpful suggestions, and provided wise counsel in book-writing and in life—Ellen Carlton, Reba Connell, Jacqueline Raphael, Jean Royson, Shufang Tsai, Mira Queen, and Linda Yamashita.

Introduction

As teachers, we see only the tip of the iceberg. There's so much about our students we don't know—where they've come from, what their home life is like, how they rank in the fierce social order of their peers. This curriculum is designed to help middle- and high-school teachers build authentic relationships with their students and help young people deepen their connection with themselves, with their classmates, and with writing.

What sets it apart from other English Language Arts curriculum is that lessons seamlessly integrate mindfulness and self-compassion exercises within them. Time-pressured teachers don't need to diverge from their mandate to teach the Common Core Standards to share mindfulness. And students build confidence and stamina to work with anxiety, boredom, irritation, and all the other emotions that inevitably arise when faced with learning tasks at school, whether they be writing assignments, exams, presentations, or simply relating with others at school.

In the first few lessons, emphasis is placed on connecting with each other and the natural world. Ironically enough, when students were given the option of working with a paper packet versus a digital one tucked away in their Google Classroom, many preferred paper. For my mostly disorganized students, unconcerned about academics or school in general, their vote for paper and pencil, though infinitely less efficient, felt like a win for cultivating embodied awareness.

In lesson two, inspired by the poem "The Summer Day" by Mary Oliver, I invited them to reflect upon the value of stepping away from their screens and connecting with the real world. One high-school student responded that by doing so, "you disconnect from others' opinions and get to sit in only your own thoughts. . . . With phones, you are constantly being shoved with others' opinions, how you should act, what to think, what's cool and who liked your post." Another student wrote about her deep connection with self in her poem "My Ocean":

My Ocean

Who made the jellyfish?
This jellyfish, I mean—
The one who has propelled itself through soft currents
The one who is silently alive
Who is flowing wherever the current takes them.
I don't know exactly what power is.

I do know how to listen to my body,
How to take care of my plants,
How to take care of myself.
Tell me, who are you living for?

—Maddy, twelfth grade

Mindfulness instructors often use the ocean as a metaphor for the mind and refer to the quiet waters of calm and clarity beneath the sometimes choppy surface of agitation, fear, and doubt. This reservoir of knowing is available if we allow ourselves to pause and take a few conscious breaths. From this relaxed state, we are more able to acknowledge whatever conflicting emotions may be present, and we turn toward ourselves with compassion. Through this cultivation of present-moment awareness, we can quiet the voices of self-criticism and self-doubt as we face the blank page or screen or any of the other myriad challenges of being a teenager (or an adult, for that matter) today.

Throughout the curriculum, the theme of self-love and self-acceptance is returned to again and again. Derek Walcott's poem "Love After Love" serves as an exemplary model. Here is one high-school student's version:

Love After Lust

The time will come when,
with contentment, you will greet yourself arriving
at your own backyard,
in your own field of sunflowers,
and each will cry at the other's welcome,
and say, "Pleasure to meet you! Come in!"
You will love again the stranger who was your self.
Give matcha. Give peaches.
Give back your heart to itself,
to the stranger who has loved you all your life,
whom you shoved
for another, who knows your devotion.
Take down the disposable pictures, the messages, the memories.
Feel the calmness after the storm.
Marinate in it.

—Sammi, eleventh grade

Another student astutely reflected on the value of practicing mindfulness and self-compassion, saying she noticed that it was the kids on campus who had the toughest lives who were the least kind to those around them.

How do we be kind? By being brave enough to look at the hurt places inside ourselves. By being willing to place our hands on our hearts, if only in our imagination, and in some small way say, "Hello. I'm here with you. You're not alone." It's from that shaky place inside where we all begin. And for the kids who believe they've got it all wrong, that God or whoever made a grave mistake in bringing them into the world, being able to connect with that feeling and express it is some sort of bread crumb on the path home.

MY STORY

My journey to mindfulness and writing arose from my own life challenges. As a child, my mother endured crippling rheumatoid arthritis and breast cancer. One brother suffered from mental illness, and another had a tragic motorcycle accident in his early twenties that left him a paraplegic. Instead of rallying around each other in our moments of pain and confusion, everyone seemed to shut down emotionally and retreat into themselves.

I spent my twenties running away, ostensibly exploring the world, though deep in my heart I came to realize that I was seeking "geographic solutions" to the anxiety and depression I felt. Yoga became a refuge, a place where I could reconnect with my body and breath and experience brief reprieves from my racing thoughts.

Since those early days on the yoga mat, mindfulness has been an enduring ally. I've been trained to drop beneath the rushing thoughts in my head and tune into the physical sensations in my body. I've learned to self-soothe by placing my hand on my heart and offering myself some gentle words of comfort. It's these simple, yet powerful skills I'm so passionate about sharing with others.

WHAT IS MINDFULNESS?

Mindfulness is developing awareness of whatever is happening right here, right now. This sense of presence is a gift, a quality we may notice in someone particularly delightful to be around. Unhurried, open, attentive—such an individual is an oasis in the desert of distraction of our modern world.

We can develop this remarkable presence of mind by anchoring our attention to sound, body sensation, or breath and allowing whatever arises in the mind to simply be there without getting carried away by it. The chatter in our heads no longer defines us. With practice, we begin to see our regrets about what happened in the past and our worries about what might happen in the future as temporary mental events, just like the sounds in the room and the breath coming into and leaving our bodies. This understanding is experiential, and though we're prone to forget, each time we bring ourselves back to the object of our attention, we remember.

WHY MINDFULNESS IN EDUCATION?

The mental health crisis facing young people today is unprecedented. In the recent U.S. Surgeon General's Advisory on Protecting Youth Mental Health, Dr. Vivek Murthy urged all sectors of society to do their part to protect the mental health of young people. He noted the severity of the problem with pre-pandemic statistics showing that one in three high school students suffered from persistent feelings of sadness and hopelessness, a 40 percent increase between 2009 and 2019, and a 57 percent jump in suicide rates for youth aged ten to twenty-four. Statistics reported by the American Psychological Association are staggering, as well: Between 2005 and 2017, there was a 52 percent increase in major depressive episodes for adolescents between the ages of twelve and seventeen. During the pandemic-related school closures, 81 percent of teens reported that they experienced negative impacts.

As Murthy reports, social media has a big role to play. And my students corroborated his findings. One high school student wrote,

> With social media, I got validation instantaneously. . . . The negative aspect of this is that I became addicted to [it] because of the dopamine hit. I wanted more and more validation, but it was never enough. I wondered what new thing I could post that would make everyone's mouth drop. . . . I was always tired and could never sleep. I couldn't focus properly and all I could think about was how I looked. . . . I literally hated myself so much during this time.

At first it may seem like a surprising response, but to deal with this crisis, we teachers must train our own minds. Young people learn to attune to their own thoughts, feelings, and behaviors in response to supportive, caring adults in their immediate environment; this is called co-regulation. Students need us to go inside and, as Neruda says in the poem "Keeping Quiet" in chapter 6, "stop waving our arms so much." They need us to pause, breathe, and cultivate our own inner sanctuary of calm and stability, so they may connect with theirs.

In my personal and professional life, I remind myself again and again that there is no day off from mindfulness, no day off from living by vow, by intention. Recently, on a Friday afternoon, when the last student smiled and waved good-bye, saying, "Have a nice weekend!" I began repeating to myself, "Stand with yourself. Whatever does or doesn't happen this weekend, stand with yourself in self-compassion. Don't go against yourself. Keep Don Miguel Ruiz's first agreement—'Be impeccable with your word.'" What strength, what confidence can come out of that! "Whatever happens, I'm not leaving." A love that's unconditional, for all times, for all situations, "good" and "bad."

HOW CURRICULUM IS ORGANIZED

Each lesson in the curriculum is centered around a poem, whose theme illustrates a positive quality such as gratitude or acceptance. A short, guided awareness practice invites students to turn their attention inward and develop their attention and self-compassion "muscles." Listening activities and poem-writing templates support students to appreciate the artistry of the poems and create their own verse. They may also choose the option of writing a personal narrative inspired by the poem. A *response to literature* paragraph, in which students connect with the poem's theme, is also included.

The sequence of lessons follows the emotional arc of the school year. In the excitement of a new school year in August and September, the themes of community and connection with the natural world are addressed (lessons 1–3). After the novelty has worn off and many students (and perhaps, yourself) slide into disillusionment and, dare I say, despair in November and

December, lessons focus on self-compassion, difficult emotions, gratitude, and letting go (lessons 4–8). In January, the renewed brightness and intention-setting is reflected in lesson 9 on habits. The focus on self widens to include others in lessons on empathy, compassion, and forgiveness in February and March (lessons 10–11). The final lesson in April, post-standardized testing, is appropriately centered around joy.

The guided mindfulness practices also build upon one another, starting with developing awareness of the body through yoga postures or simple stretching exercises, followed by a simple listening activity to support students beginning to gather their attention. All the subsequent lessons begin in a similar fashion, with gentle movements and grounding in the body, followed by opportunities to experiment with different ways of anchoring attention, such as through breath and creative visualizations. Cultivating compassion is a recurring theme throughout the lessons, which first begins with oneself, and then extends to others.

Students also hone important academic reading and writing skills as they persevere to comprehend these complex texts. Text-dependent questions ask them to use context clues to decipher unfamiliar vocabulary, demonstrate their understanding of figurative language, and make inferences. A text response paragraph writing prompt allows them to show their understanding of the poem's theme by citing textual evidence.

For English learners, the lessons provide ample listening and speaking opportunities as well as bite-sized yet challenging reading and writing tasks. Interpreting poetry demands critical analysis as well as provides students with rich terrain to explore their emotional lives and their values as they navigate coming of age in a new culture.

The challenge of writing their own poems and stories engages students in the higher-order thinking skill at the top of Bloom's Taxonomy: create. Through this process, they come to appreciate the poems on a deeper level as well as experience the joy of self-expression. Collaborating with their peers as they work through the steps of the writing process allows students to strengthen not only their writing but also their relational and communication skills required in today's team-focused workplaces.

REAPING THE BENEFITS

To see how poetry lessons grounded in mindfulness impacted my students on a socio-emotional level, I asked my English Learner students to rate their resilience through a self-compassion survey at the start of the school year and again in the spring. Dr. Kristen Neff, pioneering educational researcher, teacher, and author of the book *Self-Compassion*, created this survey to measure how we relate to ourselves when confronted with difficulties, failures, or a sense of our own inadequacies. Our result: Two-thirds of students surveyed increased in self-compassion.

The program also proved effective at developing their reading and writing skills. At midyear, 40 percent advanced to the next level of ELD (English Language Development), compared to 20 percent the previous year.

The improved academic outcomes that result from attending to students' emotional lives is well-researched. In 2011, the Collaborative for Academic, Social, and Emotional Learning (CASEL) found in a meta-analysis of 213 school-based social and emotional learning programs that students' academic performance increased by 11 percentile points, compared to students who did not participate in such programs.

FINAL NOTE

Reaching students' hearts through mindfulness practice and then encouraging them to write and share from their core allows them to feel seen and honored—to feel that their emotional lives are valid and welcome at school. As a result, they become more self-confident and motivated to engage in cognitive and interpersonal tasks. One Latina colleague remarked, "If there had been this kind of curriculum in the school system when I was growing up, I believe that I would have become more confident in myself a lot earlier in life." It is my hope that you truly enjoy co-creating this learning path with your students.

REFERENCES, RESOURCES, AND FURTHER READING

Collaborative for Academic, Social and Emotional Learning. "What Does the Research Say?" https://casel.org/fundamentals-of-sel/what-does-the-research-say (accessed October 30, 2021).

Durlak, J. A., R. P. Weissberg, A. B. Dymnicki, R. D. Taylor, and K. B. Schellinger. "The Impact of Enhancing Students' Social and Emotional Learning: A Meta-Analysis of School-Based Universal Interventions." *Child Development* 82, no. 1 (February 2011): 405–32.

Murthy, Vivek. *Protecting Youth Mental Health: The U.S. Surgeon General's Advisory*. Washington, DC: U.S. Public Health Service, 2021, www.hhs.gov/sites/default/files/surgeon-general-youth-mental-health-advisory.pdf (accessed July 29, 2022).

Neff, Kristen. *Self-Compassion*. New York: William Morrow, 2011.

———. Self-Compassion Scale—Short Form. https://self-compassion.org/wp-content/uploads/2015/02/ShortSCS.pdf.

"Stress in America 2020 Survey Signals a Growing National Mental Health Crisis." Washington, DC: American Psychological Association, 2020, www.apa.org/news/press/releases/stress/2020/sia-mental-health-crisis.pdf (accessed August 6, 2022).

Chapter One
Becoming a Mindful Educator

"Raise your words, not your voice.
It is rain that grows flowers, not thunder."

~ Rumi

Mindfulness is befriending ourselves with whatever is happening right here, right now. Watching our thoughts without deeming one "good" and clinging to it, or another "bad" and rejecting it, helps to reduce stress and reactivity and invites greater sanity into our lives. To illustrate, it may help to think of the mind as a stage in which thoughts, feelings, and sensations make an appearance and then quickly exit stage left. It would be quite liberating if we could watch this drama unfolding and say to ourselves, *What an interesting cast of characters!* The truth is that we rarely have this sense of objective awareness. We're caught up in the stream of our storylines, such as "This student doesn't like me; my colleagues think I'm incompetent; I don't belong here; I'm overwhelmed; I can't do this," and we rarely find a moment when we can rest and be at ease, let alone be entertained by it all.

In the realm of education, mindfulness is not only a way to decrease stress and improve academic outcomes, but it also builds character. By being more self-aware, we can make better choices, better decisions. Thich Nhat Hanh, renowned Buddhist monk, poet, scholar, and human rights activist, emphasizes this ethical dimension of mindfulness. In the opening pages of *Happy Teachers Change the World*, he writes: "Our mission as teachers is not just to transmit knowledge, but to form human beings, to construct a worthy, beautiful human race, in order to take care of our precious planet." His broad view of mindfulness is as a path to build happy, healthy, and compassionate learning communities grounded in love and understanding rather than as simply a tool to improve academic performance and prevent teacher burnout.

BEGINNING A PRACTICE

Tuning into our bodies is where we begin our mindfulness practice. Though the mind may be thousands of miles away, the only place the body can be is in the present moment. As such, it serves as an anchor for our practice. Tuning into sensation and the waves of breath coming and going helps to slow down the barrage of thoughts in our heads. However, the goal of mindfulness is not to stop thinking; this is a common misconception. Brains think and perceive; that's what they were designed to do. The practice is simply to be aware of what arises in our consciousness with kindness and without judgment. Though the practice is simple, mastering it can take a lifetime.

Beginning a mindfulness practice is best done in community with an experienced teacher. Sitting together with other people offers the benefit of support. Kaiser Permanente offers a free workshop series on managing stress, which includes short, guided mindfulness practices. Mindfulness-Based Stress Reduction classes (MBSR), based on the decades-old model developed by Jon Kabat-Zinn to help patients suffering from chronic pain, are also offered for a nominal fee. Check offerings from health-care providers in your local area. Online courses, such as Mindful Schools' Mindfulness Fundamentals and A Still Quiet Place, offered by Dr. Amy Saltzman, director of the Association of Mindfulness in Education, are also excellent options.

Finding colleagues interested in practicing together can be a tremendous support. Taking a few minutes to ground in the body and connect with the breath serves as a touchstone for the presence of mind we wish to bring to interactions with our students, our colleagues, and especially ourselves. It's this moment-to-moment embodiment of the practice throughout the day—how we answer the phone call interrupting a lesson, how we respond to challenging student behavior, and how we interact with other adults—that sets the example for our students.

Thank you for your willingness to be vulnerable, to take the lead in turning your attention inward. Your students will benefit from your efforts, whether or not you ever teach them mindfulness. Also, thank you for lifting up poetry. Poetry is a treasure to humanity that dignifies, enlightens, and heals. Giving students the opportunity to interact with these poems and try their own hand at a few lines plants the seeds for a more balanced life and a more beautiful world.

REFERENCES, RESOURCES, AND FURTHER READING

Brensilver, Matthew, JoAnna Hardy, and Oren Jay Sofer. *Teaching Mindfulness to Empower Adolescents.* New York: Norton, 2020.

Hanh, Thich Nhat, and Katherine Weare. *Happy Teachers Change the World*. Berkeley: Parallax, 2017.

Saltzman, Amy. *A Still Quiet Place: A Mindfulness Program for Teaching Children and Adolescents to Ease Stress and Difficult Emotions.* Oakland: New Harbinger, 2014.

Sofer, Oren Jay, and Matthew Brensilver. *The Mindful Schools Curriculum for Adolescents.* New York: Norton, 2019.

Chapter Two
Building Resiliency

“Be willing to be a beginner every single morning.”

~ Meister Eckhart

It goes without saying that if we're truly committed to being present for our students and helping them to navigate their oftentimes-turbulent inner worlds, it's critical to reflect on the impact of traumatic events in our own lives, seek counseling, and find safe places where we can bring our whole selves in community with others to heal. The understanding and compassion that arise as we learn to gently hold our own pain is what prepares us to mentor our students to hold their own. We protect ourselves from emotional fatigue or burnout and feeling overwhelmed or numb.

It's also important to educate ourselves and young people about the *window of tolerance*, a concept originally developed by Dan Siegel to describe one's internal zone of support, measured in terms of one's level of arousal. Arousal can be thought of as one's basic readiness for life—it's what gets us out of bed in the morning and enables us to navigate the world.

Trauma creates dysregulated arousal, when we lose our ability to self-regulate. This can appear in one of two ways: hyperarousal or hypoarousal. Hyperarousal, feeling anxious and easily overwhelmed, is when there's too much energy in the system; hypoarousal, when there's not enough, leaves us feeling unmotivated, disinterested, and numb. Staying in the sweet spot between these two extremes is what allows our arousal to ebb and flow based on stimulation from our surroundings and our internal experience, and to feel present, relaxed, and engaged.

This is why helping our students tune into their moment-to-moment internal experience is so important: It helps them remain within their window of tolerance. By cultivating their self-awareness in this way and making connections between their thoughts, emotions, and bodily sensations, they develop the tools to practice self-care as they learn mindfulness.

In his book *Trauma-Sensitive Mindfulness*, David Treleaven offers many helpful suggestions. To create a safe “container,” or practice environment for students, it's important to keep them in the driver's seat. Provide various options for practice, such as keeping their eyes open, grounding in their hands and feet, or noticing sights and sounds in their surroundings, rather than strictly focusing on their internal experience. If necessary, they may opt out of a practice altogether. Keep practices brief (under ten minutes), as the guided-practice scripts suggest.

Be sure to leave sufficient time after a practice for students to talk about what they noticed and normalize a wide range of experiences. For students who may have been captured by a traumatic memory, intense emotion, or body sensation, ask grounding questions tied to the five senses to help bring them back to the present moment. One effective practice is the 5-4-3-2-1 Calming Technique. Ask students to notice five things they can see, four things they can touch, three things they can hear, two things they can smell, and one thing they can taste.

Remind them of the people they can go to for support and refer a student who may have been triggered by a practice to a school counselor or therapist, if possible. However, it's important to note that sending a student to see a mental health provider may not be a viable option; there just aren't enough counselors to go around. According to the American Counseling Association, the average school counselor in public schools has a roster of 455 students. This nearly doubles their recommended ratio of 250:1. In states like California, the ratio is 663 to 1.

Ultimately, discussion of "trauma-informed" practice can be a double-edged sword. On the one hand, it's certainly good to be aware of the possible problems that looking inward can bring up. On the other hand, the vast majority of kids are quite resilient, and the emphasis on trauma may cause you, the educator, some anxiety, trying to bring mindfulness to your class. Press forward by keeping practices short, and by giving kids options, like those mentioned in this chapter. And certainly keep an eye on those with significant mental or behavioral issues.

Particularly for those of us working within the public education system, gaining an understanding of systemic oppression is also key. We must inquire into our relative positions of privilege in terms of age, social class, gender, sexual orientation, ethnicity and national origin, religion, and ability. Reflecting on our social location and the relative privilege we've been afforded because of it is an essential part of our own healing and ability to serve as role models for our students.

REFERENCES, RESOURCES, AND FURTHER READING

Bray, Bethany. "One School Counselor per 455 Students: Nationwide Average Improves." American Counseling Association, May 10, 2019, https://ct.counseling.org/2019/05/one-school-counselor-per-455-students-nationwide-average-improves (accessed August 1, 2022).

MTV. "How We Cope with Anxiety and Stress: MTV's Teen Code." Educational video, 7:09. March 12, 2020, www.youtube.com/watch?v=0qnYXCLk5bQ (accessed August 1, 2022).

Siegel, Dan. *Mindsight: The New Science of Personal Transformation.* New York: Bantam Books, 2010.

Treleaven, David. *Trauma-Sensitive Mindfulness.* New York: Norton, 2018.

Van Der Kolk, Bessel. *The Body Keeps the Score: Brain, Mind, and Body in the Healing of Trauma*. New York: Penguin, 2014.

Chapter Three

Anatomy of a Mindful Writing Lesson

“Here is my secret: I don’t mind what happens.”

~ Krishnamurti

This curriculum is primarily a tool for teaching creative writing to middle- and high-school students. Each lesson is centered around an anchor poem and includes a script for a short, guided awareness practice that reinforces the theme and encourages students to relax, reflect, and write from a more open, creative place. Listening activities support students’ appreciation of the poems and build vocabulary. Then they create their own poems with the support of a template, or they may choose to write a personal narrative inspired by the theme.

Each lesson is robust and includes quick write prompts, questions for discussions, text-dependent questions, a brief section on related neuroscience and psychology, prompts to write a response to a literature paragraph, and extension activities; together they could serve as the basis for a full week of instruction. Lessons may also be tailored for delivery in a ninety-minute block or two fifty-minute sessions. They are suitable for English, English Language Development, or Special Education classes, and they could also be used in electives such as Creative Writing, Leadership, Personal Reflections, and Advisory, or serve as a creative intervention in small-group therapy settings.

To begin the lesson, encourage students to do a quick write on a question related to the theme of the poem. Next, lead the awareness practice using the script provided or your own words. Each guided practice is followed by a few questions to encourage students to talk about their experience and acknowledge common challenges, such as feeling sleepy, restless, distracted, or perhaps even irritated. A low-risk conversation starter is to ask for a show of hands of those who noticed any of these feelings or sensations arise. While many students often report feeling more relaxed afterward, it is important to normalize a wide range of experiences.

Also included in each lesson is a brief “Did You Know” section, which presents information from current research studies in neurobiology and psychology that support the efficacy of mindfulness. This section is designed primarily to introduce you to some foundational scientific concepts and boost your confidence in the practice, though it could be shared with students in developmentally appropriate ways.

Next, read the poem out loud while students listen with their eyes closed. This honors the oral tradition of poetry and allows them to visualize and appreciate the sensual details. Following on the heels of the mindfulness practice, students will be in an ideal, open, receptive frame of mind. Alternatively, you could share a YouTube video of the poet reading the poem or a more creative visual interpretation of it.

Provide students with the cloze-listening worksheet, which draws their attention to the poem's more challenging vocabulary and allows them to hear it a second time; the rich, condensed poetic language merits multiple readings. A small-group option is for a student leader to read the poem aloud while their peers complete the worksheet. In classes with English learners, you may like to ask a volunteer to read a translation of the poem (or in some cases, the works in their original language).

Afterward, invite students to share what they notice and appreciate about the poem, what feels "lit up" for them. Adopting this kind of intuitive, celebratory approach takes them into the poem and emphasizes enjoyment rather than mere academic understanding. As the poetry teacher John Brehm remarked, "Anyone can notice and appreciate. It requires no literary training; indeed, literary training is often an obstacle, as concepts and interpretive strategies can obscure the immediacy of our connection with a poem." Students can express their appreciation by highlighting favorite words or phrases. Another simple entry point is to ask them to identify ten concrete nouns. This heightens their awareness of specificity, a hallmark of good writing, in general, and what makes poetry so imagistic and evocative.

Text-dependent questions related to vocabulary, *figurative language* and other poetic tools, and *theme* encourage students to appreciate the poet's craft. A personal reflection question invites them to reflect upon how the poem's message is relevant to their own lives.

To boost student confidence as they begin writing a poem, you may choose to gather everyone's ideas in a playful, collaborative class poem. Next, provide one of the versions of the writing play sheets. With varying degrees of scaffolding, they highlight the structure of the original poem and invite students to substitute their own concrete imagery. More advanced writers may also simply free-write, beginning with a favorite line. This draft can later be revised, edited, and broken into lines, if desired.

A WORD ON QUICK WRITES

The mind is quick, so you need a quick pen to capture it. Natalie Goldberg, famed writing instructor and Zen student, recommends the Pilot 7 fountain pen. She likes pen and paper, as well as the textural nature of longhand, which requires the engagement of both body and mind, much like mindfulness practice. And like mindfulness practice, writing practice is timed. This helps to keep you on task, when your inner critic, born of fear and judgment, wishes you would stop. You may choose to start small and add minutes later. But you must commit to whatever time you've chosen for that session.

Here are Goldberg's Rules of Writing Practice from *Writing Down the Bones*:

1. *Keep your hand moving.* (Don't pause to reread the line you have just written. That's stalling and trying to get control of what you're saying.)
2. *Don't cross out.* (That is editing as you write. Even if you write something you didn't mean to write, leave it as it is.)
3. *Don't worry about spelling, punctuation, or grammar.* (Don't even care about staying within the margins and lines on the page.)
4. *Lose control.*
5. *Don't think. Don't get logical.*
6. *Go for the jugular.* (If something comes up in your writing that is scary or naked, dive right into it. It probably has lots of energy.)

So much of mindfulness practice is about watering the seeds of self-compassion, and a favorite addendum to Goldberg's original list is the seventh rule: "I am free to write the worst junk in the world." Nonjudgmental awareness is what we cultivate in mindfulness practice—to be equanimous with all that arises in the phenomenal world, and in our own consciousness. Humans are quick to judge everything and everyone: "Is this good or bad? Are they a friend or a foe?" In mindful writing practice, we start with ourselves, with our own words. We practice acknowledging what's present in the mind—the first, fresh, uncensored thought, naked and raw, allowing it to be there, and then embracing it.

Along with compassionate acceptance, writing practice also demands bravery, commitment, and determination. You must be fierce to write past the censor, to keep your hand moving and allow yourself to lose control. That's not what the ego wants. The ego wants to feel solid ground beneath it. But actually it's not ground; it's a fireball. So, dance! Move! Keep your hand moving. Goldberg points out, "In writing, when you are truly on, there's no writer, no paper, no pen, no thoughts. Only writing does writing—everything else is gone."

WORKING WITH ENGLISH LEARNERS AND SPECIAL EDUCATION STUDENTS

The reading, writing, and social-emotional learning skills these lessons address are relevant for all populations of students at the secondary level. Below are a few suggestions of how to help make them more accessible to both English learners and other students needing extra support.

- Have students read poems out loud in their native tongues. This fortifies their pride in their language and culture, as well as their self-esteem.
- Amplify the curriculum by creating a slide deck that presents individual stanzas accompanied by visual aids and basic comprehension questions.
- Generate word banks together, from which students may choose ideas to complete their poems.

- Use the basic writing play sheets to encourage students to draw pictures and complete sentence starters.

REFERENCES, RESOURCES, AND FURTHER READING

Goldberg, Natalie. *Writing Down the Bones.* Boston: Shambhala, 1986.

Nye, Naomi Shihab. "One Boy Told Me," Geraldine R. Dodge Poetry Festival. Video of poetry reading, 2:37. Uploaded March 30, 2009. www.youtube.com/watch?v=biJ3FP8aDjY (accessed August 1, 2022).

Lesson One

Creating a Practice Community

"Give a Little Love" by Charlie Fink

"When we live only the life of a wave and are not able to live the life of water, we suffer quite a lot."

~ Thich Nhat Hanh

OBJECTIVES

Mindfulness Skills	Practice mindful movement through a series of simple standing yoga poses
CASEL Competencies Highlights	Relationship skills: Developing positive relationships Responsible decision-making: reflecting on one's role to promote community well-being
Creative Writing Task (Aligns with CCSS.ELA-LITERACY.W.9-10.3 a-e; W.9-10.4-6; L.9-10.1 a,b; L.9-10.2 a-c; L.9-10.3 a; ELD Part I, C, 10, 12 and ELD Part II, A-C)	Compose a song verse or personal narrative
Academic Writing Task (Aligns with CCSS.ELA-LITERACY.W.9-10.1; W.9-10.4-6; L.9-10.1 a, b; L.9-10.2 a-c; L.9-10.3 a; ELD Part I, C, 11, 12 and ELD Part II, A-C)	Analyze theme and its development in song

INTRODUCTION

Laying a strong foundation of safety and mutual respect is an important prerequisite to beginning a successful mindful writing practice with students. Finding the commonality despite race, nationality, or neighborhood is key. Why are we here together? What do we want to create based on our common beliefs about what is important? And how can something as intimidating and highbrow as poetry help?

The tools of poetry are all around us—in the thirty-second ads we see on YouTube, in the pithy and engaging phrases on our T-shirts, and on billboards in our neighborhoods. Poetry's concision, lyricism, and emphasis on sensual details also peppers the song lyrics students turn to for refuge in a sometimes bewildering, lonely, and turbulent world. So here is where we begin our journey.

A successful tool for inspiring collaboration and a sense of community is the song "Give a Little Love" by Charlie Fink. It addresses life and death, heartbreak and love, and one of the most challenging aspects of poetry: figurative language. In the song's imaginative lines—"my heart is bigger than the earth," "my love surrounds you like an ether," and "I will always be the sun and moon to you," the songwriter expresses some of the "big emotions" teens feel. The final refrain in the song—"And if you share (with your heart)/Yeah, you give (with your heart)/What you share with the world is what it keeps of you"—leaves listeners with a powerful message to contribute in a positive way to their community.

DID YOU KNOW? THE SOCIAL ENGAGEMENT SYSTEM

The foundation of learning is feeling safe and attuned to the environment, the teacher, and one's peers. In terms of our nervous system, this means that we're not on the defensive, either fighting or fleeing (sympathetic response) or shutting down (parasympathetic response). The sweet spot in the middle is part of the third type of nervous system response: the social engagement system.

Stephen Porges's polyvagal theory stemmed from his investigation into the two branches of the vagus nerve: the dorsal or posterior branch (DV) and the ventral or anterior branch (VV). Both branches serve to relax the body but in radically different ways. The dorsal branch, part of the oldest reptilian part of the autonomic nervous system (ANS), is responsible for the shutdown. The ventral branch, part of the newest part of the ANS, supports the social engagement system. The ventral vagal branch enervates head and neck muscles and the inner ear, and it helps us pick up social cues and read facial expressions. Porges coined the vagus nerve the "love" nerve because it is only present in mammals and it allows us to approach others in trusting, affectionate, and cooperative ways. To perform altruistic acts like those observed in the suggested music video is not just a higher-order character trait but an integral part of our nervous system.

STUDENT LESSON OBJECTIVES

- ✔ Become more aware of your body through yoga or simple stretches
- ✔ Think about what it takes to form healthy relationships and a strong sense of community
- ✔ Do a close reading of the song "Give a Little Love" by Charlie Fink and answer questions about it
- ✔ Write your own verse to the song or a story inspired by it
- ✔ Write a paragraph sharing what you think the songwriter's message is and share lines from the song that reflect that message

Step 1: Quick Write (5 min.) and Partner Share (5 min.)

Prompt: What is one of your best qualities or one you would like to develop this year?

Step 2: Yoga (10 min.)

Teacher Note: Begin with a few simple standing yoga postures to give students a break from their desks. Invite them to more fully inhabit their bodies and prepare to sit still. The body is a great teaching tool to develop present-moment awareness, as the present moment is the only place the body can be. Feel free to modify and remind students (and yourself) to listen to their own bodies. And if the idea of yoga poses seems too complicated, a simplified stretching routine follows the poses. (Some variations of these movements are included at the beginning of the mindfulness practice in each lesson.) While students may seem hesitant at first to engage their bodies outside of a physical education class, modeling a connection with the body throughout the day is important, and eventually many will give in to the temptation.

Mountain Pose

Stand as you are able and allow your feet to be hip-width apart. Roll the shoulders back and down and move the head from side to side, making sure the shoulders are over the hips and the hips are over the feet. Now, press the feet into the floor and lengthen the spine. Breathe in and breathe out. Enjoy the strength and stability of this pose.

Sun Breath

Now, breathing in, reach your arms out to the side and lift them up to the sky, stretching through the fingertips, and then, on the exhale, relax them back down. Do this three times together.

Spinal Twist

Again, stand with your feet comfortably apart and twist the upper torso from side to side, allowing your arms to swing like old ropes, tapping your shoulders with your hands. Follow with your head and neck. Release any tension in the spine.

Side Body Stretch

Then, breathe in and reach arms overhead. Gently pull on the left wrist, stretching through the ribs and lengthening through the left side of the body, and then do the same on the right side. Then return to mountain pose and take a grounding belly breath.

Tree Pose

From mountain pose, stand with feet hip-width apart and shift weight onto the right foot, while bringing the left foot to the right ankle, below or above the knee (not directly on the knee to prevent possible injury), or to the top of the thigh, and balance on one leg. Focus your attention on a stable point in front of you and hold the pose for a few breaths. Feel free to keep one hand on a desk or the back of a chair for support. (Pause.) *Then, return to mountain pose and pause for a breath. When you're ready, balance on the second leg.*

Chair Pose

On the inhalation, slowly bend your knees and sit back and down, as if you were about to sit in a chair while raising your arms overhead. Broadening through the chest, lift the torso and engage the lower belly. Breathe and enjoy this strengthening pose.

Forward Bend

Round your back on the inhalation; then bend your knees and allow your head to hang freely, releasing any tension. Fold your arms at the elbows and swing gently from side to side; then slowing stack the vertebra one at a time with your head coming up last. Return to mountain pose.

Now, take three community breaths together. Breathe in and breathe out. Take a full breath in and out. In and out. And as you end your practice, bring your full attention to the sound of the bell, from the very beginning to the very end, when the bell is still. (Ring bell and pause until it's silent.) Notice how you feel.

Simplified Stretching Routine

These can be done either standing or seated.

1. *Roll the head from side to side, drop the chin to the chest and lengthen through the sides of the neck.*
2. *Interlace the fingers behind the head, and on the inhale, extend the elbows out to the sides and look up at the sky, lengthening through the chest and dropping the shoulder blades. Then on the exhalation, drop the chin to the chest and gently lengthen through the cervical vertebra.*
3. *Roll the shoulders back and down and drop the head from side to side.*
4. *Drape an arm over the head and gently encourage the ear to drop to the shoulder without raising the shoulder to meet it. Extend the opposite arm to the side, pushing through the palm and extending through the fingertips.*
5. *Hold the elbow with one hand and gently extend the other down the back while looking forward.*
6. *Circle the wrists and ankles; then stretch the fingers backward and forward and finish by flickering them like twinkling stars.*
7. *Bring the forearm to the outside of the knee and twist the spine. Repeat on the other side.*
8. *Settle into stillness for a moment and notice how you feel.*

Step 3: Debrief (partners, then whole class, 5–10 min.)

1. How does your body feel?
2. What emotions or feelings came up around doing physical exercises in class?
3. Did you notice any tightness or pain in your body? Where?

Step 4: Music Video "Give a Little Love" (by Noah and the Whale, 5 min.)

Teacher Note: Ask students to notice what feelings or sensations arise in their bodies while viewing the video.

Step 5: Making Connections (5–10 min.)

1. What feelings or sensations did you notice?
2. What images stand out in your mind?
3. What message does the music video convey?

Step 6: Cloze Listening Activity (Handout A) (10 min.)

Distribute the listening worksheet and, after reviewing unfamiliar vocabulary, watch the video a second time while students complete the worksheet.

Step 7: Text-Dependent Questions (Handout B; Answers on Handout C) (15–20 min.)

Distribute Handout B for students to complete questions, either alone, with a partner, or in small groups.

Step 8: Text Response (Handout B; Sample Response on Handout C)

Prompt: The first stanza of the song says, "All is fleeting/Yeah, but all is good." How do we live "the good life"? What do you think the songwriter's message (theme) is?

Explain RAPS Strategy or similar mnemonic for this and all subsequent text-response tasks.

RAPS Strategy

- *Restate* the question by turning it into a statement.
- *Answer* all questions in the prompt.
- Provide *proof* of your thinking by adding quotes from the poem and explaining what they show.
- End by *summing up* your thinking.

Step 9: Self-Reflection (Handout B)

Prompt: Do you think giving love and being generous create happiness? Why or why not?

Step 10: Songwriting (Handout D) (10–15 min.)

Distribute Handout D, E, or F, depending on students' fluency in English and creative writing experience.

Step 11: Prose Writing Option

Prompt: Write about a time you helped a stranger or a time you wish you had.

TAKEAWAY

Cultivating character and a loving heart are visible in our actions. Taking a few moments to practice self-care helps us to more fully appreciate the moment and consider what is good to do now, before the moment is gone.

EXTENSION

Ask students to reflect upon what kind of community they would like to be part of and what makes them feel safe at school. Examples of what students may write include not being laughed at by their peers and being listened to. These notes can be used to design their own classroom posters, which will send a powerful message early on that the class will be co-created.

Give a Little Love
by Charlie Fink

Well, I know my death will not come
'til I breathe all the air out my lungs
'til my final tune is sung
that all is fleeting
5 yeah, but all is good
and my love is my whole being
and I've shared what I could
but if you give a little love, you can get a little love of your own
don't break his heart
10 yeah, if you give a little love, you can get a little love of your own
don't break his heart

Well, my heart is bigger than the earth
and though life is what gave it love first
life is not all that it's worth
15 'cause life is fleeting
yeah, but I love you
and my love surrounds you like an ether
in everything that you do
but if you give a little love, you can get a little love of your own
20 don't break his heart
yeah, if you give a little love, you can get a little love of your own
don't break his heart

yeah, if you give a little love, you can get a little love of your own
don't break his heart
25 yeah, if you give a little love, you can get a little love of your own
don't break his heart
Well, if you are (what you love)
and you do (what you love)
I will always be the sun and moon to you
30 and if you share (with your heart)
yeah, you give (with your heart)
what you share with the world is what it keeps of you

Handout A

Cloze Listening Activity

Name: ______________________________

Listen to the song and use the words to fill in the blanks.

Lungs	own	death	breathe	sung	fleeting	keeps
Life	being	shared	love	break	earth	good
Gave	worth	surrounds	sun	moon	give	

Give a Little Love
by Noah and the Whale

Well, I know my (1) ________________ will not come
'til I (2) ________________ all the air out my (3) ________________
'til my final tune is (4) ________________
that all is (5) ________________
5 yeah, but all is (6) ________________
and my (7) ________________ is my whole (8) ________________
and I've (9) ________________ what I could
but if you give a little love, you can get a little love of your (10) ________________
don't (11) ________________ his heart
10 yeah, if you give a little love, you can get a little love of your own
don't break his heart

Well, my heart is bigger than the (12) ________________
and though life is what (13) ________________ it love first
(14) ________________ is not all that it's (15) ________________
15 'cause life is fleeting
yeah, but I love you
and my love (16) ________________ you like an ether
in everything that you do
but if you give a little love, you can get a little love of your own

Continued on next page

HANDOUT A 2 / 2

20 don't break his heart
yeah, if you give a little love, you can get a little love of your own
don't break his heart
yeah, if you give a little love, you can get a little love of your own
don't break his heart
25 yeah, if you give a little love, you can get a little love of your own
don't break his heart
Well, if you are (what you love)
and you do (what you love)
I will always be the (17) _______________ and (18) _______________ to you
30 and if you share (with your heart)
yeah, you (19) _______________ (with your heart)
what you share with the world is what it (20) _______________ of you

Handout B

Text-Dependent Questions, Text Response, and Personal Reflection

Name: ______________________________

Text-Dependent Questions

1. What words surrounding the word *fleeting* in line 4 help us to understand its meaning? (context clues)

____

____

2. Why does the songwriter say that "all is fleeting"?

____

____

3. Several comparisons to the natural world (similes/metaphors) are made in the song. One example is "Well, my heart is bigger than the earth." Find two more comparisons.

____

____

4. What can you guess (infer) about the songwriter's love through these comparisons?

____

____

5. In line 14, the songwriter says, "Life is not all that it's worth," suggesting (implying) that life can be challenging. How does he find purpose in his life?

____

____

6. Using rhyme and repeating words (repetition) creates rhythm. An example of rhyming words is "lungs and sung." Find another example of rhyme and an example of repetition.

____

____

Continued on next page

Text Response

Examine the theme of the song and its development. Cite textual evidence.

Prompt

The first stanza of the song says, "all is fleeting/Yeah, but all is good." How do we live "the good life"? What do you think the songwriter's message (theme) is?

Self-Reflection

Do you think giving love and being generous create happiness? Why or why not? Give an example from your life.

Handout C

Text-Dependent Questions Answer Key and Sample Text Response

Text-Dependent Questions Answer Key

1. Death, final tune
2. Because he is aware that sooner or later, he and everyone else will die.
3. "My love surrounds you like an ether"; "I will always be the sun and moon to you"
4. His love is boundless and good.
5. By participating fully and giving of himself to others.
6. Rhyme: good/could; repetition of refrain: "But if you give a little love, you can get a little love of your own/Don't break his heart."

Teacher Note: Encourage students to explore their previous experiences and arrive at their own conclusions. For many, giving love may have not had good outcomes. This is true of personal relationships, whether with family members, friends, or significant others. For students of color who are subject to systemic racism, LGBTQ+, handicapped, and other minority students, there are other layers of pain and suffering to acknowledge. Encourage everyone to acknowledge their own truths while not forgetting the inspiring message of the song.

Sample Text Response

The theme of the song "Give a Little Love" is to be generous and altruistic. Because the songwriter is so aware of the impermanence of all things (including ourselves), he doesn't hold back from loving completely. In the lines of the first stanza, he writes, "All is fleeting/ yeah, but all is good/and my love is my whole being/and I've shared what I could." By moving beyond a small, contracted, and fearful self and recognizing that we're not alone on this planet, we're able to leave something behind as a legacy: "what you share with the world is what it keeps of you."

Handout D

Songwriting Play Sheet

Name: ______________________________

Copy your favorite line from the song "Give a Little Love" below:

____

____

Next, brainstorm a list of three to five things in each category:

Huge Things	Impermanent Things	Invisible Things

Now use ideas from your lists to write your own verse for the song:

Well, my heart is bigger than __________________________
(something huge)

And though life is like ___________________________________
(something impermanent)

My love surrounds you like ____________________________
(something invisible)

In everything that you do.

Continued on next page

Draw a picture to go along with your verse.

CREATIVE WRITING EXAMPLES

Song Lyric Example

Well, my heart is bigger than my pockets
and although life is like a tank of gas,
my love surrounds you like the fragrance of jasmine
in everything that you do.

—Edgar, twelfth grade

Free-Writing Example (after copying a favorite line)

My love is my whole being and I've shared what I could.
My love is every hair on my head
every beat of my heart
every breath I take
every word I write
every thought I think
every dish I wash
every pile of cat vomit I wipe up
every whistle of the freight trains
every tinkle of the wind chimes
every thought to reach out
and then pull back in fear
every thought that I'm completely alone
that I'm an island unto myself
that nothing will ever change
that there's no getting better
that love isn't real
tossed around on the sea of life
intentionally moving toward rough water
seeking it out
when I can hardly breathe
I can hardly breathe

—Laura Bean (author)

Prose

An example of a time when I was kind was when I bought food for someone without knowing them well. We were on a field trip and went into Starbucks for lunch. Everyone was ordering, but my classmate forgot his money. He looked awkward and embarrassed, so I paid for his chicken panini and Frappuccino. He got a good lunch, and someone was kind to him without asking for anything in return. It reminded me how loving I can be, not just with people I know, but others I don't.

—Sheila, eleventh grade

One time I didn't help and wish I had was when I was fifteen or sixteen years old, working at my father's ice cream store. This very old, frail woman came up to the counter and ordered one scoop of vanilla ice cream in a plain cone. She was very quiet and, I soon surmised, without funds. I don't remember if she even spoke. What I do remember was the softness in her eyes, pleading with me to give her that ice cream cone that sat on the stainless-steel counter and began to melt. The question became which would melt sooner—the ice cream or my heart. All I remember is finally returning the ice cream to the tub from which it had come. I probably smiled and laughed nervously. I don't know what I did. But almost forty years later, I still remember the time I only saw in black and white.

—Laura Bean (author)

REFERENCES, RESOURCES, AND FURTHER READING

Noah and the Whale. "Give a Little Love." YouTube video, 4:35. December 2, 2012. www.youtube.com/watch?v=y0abYKwRWIU (accessed August 1, 2022).

Porges, Stephen. *Polyvagal Theory.* New York: Norton, 2011.

Wagner, Dee. "Polyvagal Theory in Practice." June 27, 2016. https://ct.counseling.org/2016/06/polyvagal-theory-practice (accessed August 1, 2022).

Lesson Two

The Gift of Attention

"The Summer Day" by Mary Oliver

" Because true belonging only happens when we present our authentic, imperfect selves to the world, our sense of belonging can never be greater than our level of self-acceptance. "

~ Brené Brown

OBJECTIVES

Mindfulness Skills	Practice focusing and grounding attention
CASEL Competencies Highlight	Self-awareness: develop interests and a sense of purpose
Creative Writing Task (Aligns with CCSS.ELA-LITERACY.W.9-10.3 a-e; W.9-10.4-6; L.9-10.1 a,b; L.9-10.2 a-c; L.9-10.3 a; ELD Part I, C, 10, 12 and ELD Part II, A-C)	Create a poem or personal narrative detailing a moment of presence
Academic Writing Task (Aligns with CCSS.ELA-LITERACY.W.9-10.1; W.9-10.4-6; L.9-10.1 a, b; L.9-10.2 a-c; L.9-10.3 a; ELD Part I, C, 11, 12 and ELD Part II, A-C)	Analyze theme and its development in poem

INTRODUCTION

Students are often told to pay attention but are rarely trained how. Just like we do reps to gain physical strength, refocusing our attention again and again trains our muscle of awareness. In Mary Oliver's poem "The Summer Day," the speaker illustrates an effortless, mindful curiosity by falling into the grass to commune with a grasshopper. Here she looks deeply into the complicated eyes of her companion and reflects on what she values most. It's this kind of embodied, gentle exploration we invite our students to bring to the practice of observing the thoughts and feelings that pass through their minds.

DID YOU KNOW? TRAUMA-INFORMED AND HEALING-CENTERED MINDFULNESS

Trauma is ubiquitous in our society. According to conservative estimates from the Centers for Disease Control and Prevention, one in seven children was the victim of child abuse and neglect in 2019; this percentage is five times higher for children in low-income households. One in four girls and one in thirteen boys have experienced sexual abuse. While mindfulness practice can support students' focus and emotional regulation, it's important to be alert to instances in which our best intentions can leave students feeling bad about themselves, that they have failed, or, in the worst case, retraumatized. As mentioned in the notes on building resiliency in chapter 2, be sure to keep practices brief and provide options such as keeping their eyes open, choosing an anchor of attention that is stabilizing and supportive (which may be sights or sounds rather than the body or breath), or opting out of the practice altogether and sitting at the back of the room to simply take a break, quietly color, or read. It's important to debrief with students after a practice and to normalize a wide range of experiences.

STUDENT LESSON OBJECTIVES

- ✔ Practice mindful listening
- ✔ Practice the 5-4-3-2-1 grounding technique to stay calm and grounded when you feel anxious
- ✔ Be more aware of what interests you and what's important to you
- ✔ Do a close reading of the poem "The Summer Day" by Mary Oliver and answer questions about it
- ✔ Write your own version of the poem or a story inspired by it
- ✔ Write a paragraph sharing what you think the poet's message is and find lines from the poem to support your ideas

Step 1: Quick Write (5 min.) and Partner Share (5 min.)

Option 1: A Memory

Prompt: Zero in on five good minutes from your summer, connecting with an animal or something from nature.

Option 2: An Experience

Prompt: Spend five good minutes outside the classroom observing something in the natural world. It could be a leaf, a flower, an insect, or the sky. Open up all your senses to record color, texture, sound, smell, and anything else you notice about it, as if you were a scientist and had never seen anything like it before.

Step 2: Guided Practice (7–10 min.)

Teacher Note: For this opening mindfulness practice, introduce the mindfulness bell or chime (or preferably, a Vibratone for its secularity). Reserve this object only for practice and train students to ring the bell at the beginning and end of the practice. Encourage them to ground themselves with a deep inhalation and exhalation before "inviting" the sound.

Script

Practicing mindfulness means intentionally slowing down. You might be asking yourself, Why would I ever want to do that? *Doesn't your life seem to be about catching up on homework, keeping your commitments outside of school, and spending any extra time on your never-ending social media feeds? Yet there's something to be gained by hitting the pause button now and again. Building our capacity to be aware of what's happening both inside us and around us in the present moment can help us to relax, be more self-aware, and reconnect with our basic goodness, as well as avoid making rash decisions and acting impulsively.*

So, let's practice being right here, right now, and bringing our full attention to just one thing—listening to the sound of the bell. (Ring bell.) *Now I'm going to ring the bell a second time and ask you to bring your full attention to the sound from the very beginning to the very end; then raise your hand when you no longer hear it.* (Ring bell and acknowledge hands raised at the end.) *Now this last time, I invite you to be aware of any thoughts that pop up in your mind, or any feelings or sensations in your body. Just be curious about what arises while you're doing this one thing—listening to the sound of the bell.* (Poll students at the end.) *Raise your hand if you were aware of a thought. Who was aware of a feeling? A sensation?*

The job of the mind is to think and feel, so don't judge yourself if you got distracted from just practicing listening. In fact, noticing when something comes up is, in itself, a moment of awareness, so, good job, everyone!

Now I'd like to invite you to quietly observe your surroundings. (Pause.) *Notice five things you can see, four things you can hear, three things you can touch, two things you can smell, and one thing you can taste.* (Pause for 1–2 minutes.) *This is a grounding practice you can choose to do anytime you'd like to support you to stay present and relaxed in your body.* (Ring bell to end the practice.)

Step 3: Debrief (partners, then whole class, 5–10 min.)

Teacher Note: For this and all subsequent post-mindfulness discussions, it's important to let go of expectations. It may be difficult for students to articulate much about their mindfulness experiments. If so, polling students with a show of hands of who saw "x" or who felt "y" or who thought about "z" is an easy alternative. This is also a useful tool in helping to normalize a wide range of experiences. Then move on to Step 4. Students will be receptive to the words of the poem in this relaxed and open environment.

1. What did you see? hear? touch? smell? taste?
2. How did it feel to listen to the bell?
3. Were you aware of any thoughts or feelings that came up? Would you like to share what you noticed?

Step 4: Read "The Summer Day"

Read poem aloud. Encourage students to visualize what they hear.

Step 5: Making Connections (5–10 min.)

1. What do you like about the poem?
2. What images stand out in your mind?
3. What words or phrases do you remember?

Step 6: Cloze Listening Activity (Handout A) (10 min.)

Discuss and sort words in text box by parts of speech. Then read the poem aloud a second time, pausing while students fill in the missing words.

Step 7: Text-Dependent Questions (Handout B; Answers on Handout C) (15–20 min.)

Distribute Handout B for students to complete questions, either alone, with a partner, or in small groups.

Step 8: Text Response (Handout B; Sample Response on Handout C)

Prompt: At the end of the poem, Oliver asks, "What is it you plan to do with your one wild and precious life?" What is she urging us to do?

Step 9: Self-Reflection (Handout B)

Prompt: What is the value of stepping away from our screens and connecting with the real world? How are you managing your "digital life"?

Step 10: Poem Writing (Handout D, E, or F) (10–15 min.)

Distribute Handout D, E, or F, depending on students' fluency in English and creative writing experience.

Step 11: Prose Writing Option

Prompt: Expand upon your quick write observing an animal or insect. What do you wonder about this creature? What might it teach you about life? What thoughts, feelings, or sensations do you notice as you slow down to pay attention and interact with it?

TAKEAWAY

Dropping out of the thinking mind and into the body is the truest form of homecoming. While the distance is small, the journey can be long. Fortunately, support for our practice is all around us in the natural world. And our brains and bodies are connected with the natural world—we wouldn't survive long without oxygen or water, and so on.

EXTENSION

A walking meditation is another way to encourage students to more fully inhabit their bodies. To begin the practice, invite them to sink their attention into their feet, and with eyes open but softly focused, begin to slowly walk. Each step taken with awareness reminds them of the support of the earth beneath them. Adding simple phrases, which they may silently repeat to themselves, helps them to train their focus and block out other worries and distractions. One is "One breath, one step." As they inhale, they say the words "one breath" as they lift a foot, and then "one step" as they exhale and place it on the ground. Another is to say "I am here" with one step and "I am home" with the next, which reminds them that, at the deepest level, they belong on this earth.

The Summer Day
by Mary Oliver

Who made the world?
Who made the swan, and the black bear?
Who made the grasshopper?
This grasshopper, I mean—
5 the one who has flung herself out of the grass,
the one who is eating sugar out of my hand,
who is moving her jaws back and forth instead of up and down—
who is gazing around with her enormous and complicated eyes.
Now she lifts her pale forearms and thoroughly washes her face.
10 Now she snaps her wings open, and floats away.
I don't know exactly what a prayer is.
I do know how to pay attention, how to fall down
into the grass, how to kneel in the grass,
how to be idle and blessed, how to stroll through the fields,
15 which is what I have been doing all day.
Tell me, what else should I have done?
Doesn't everything die at last, and too soon?
Tell me, what is it you plan to do
with your one wild and precious life?

Handout A

Cloze Listening Activity

Name: ______________________________

Sort the words below by parts of speech.

stroll	precious	flung	thoroughly	snaps	attention	kneel
grasshopper	gazing	idle	jaws	swan		

Adjective	Noun	Verb	Adverb

Continued on next page

Now listen to the poem and use the words to fill in the blanks.

The Summer Day
by Mary Oliver

Who made the world?
Who made the (1) _____________, and the black bear?
Who made the (2) _____________?
This grasshopper, I mean—
5 the one who has (3) _____________ herself out of the grass,
the one who is eating sugar out of my hand,
who is moving her (4) _____________ back and forth instead of up and down—
who is (5) _____________ around with her enormous and complicated eyes.
Now she lifts her pale forearms and (6) _____________ washes her face.
10 Now she (7) _____________ her wings open, and floats away.
I don't know exactly what a prayer is.
I do know how to pay (8) _____________, how to fall down
into the grass, how to (9) _____________ in the grass,
how to be (10) _____________ and blessed, how to (11) _____________ through the fields,
15 which is what I have been doing all day.
Tell me, what else should I have done?
Doesn't everything die at last, and too soon?
Tell me, what is it you plan to do
with your one wild and (12) _____________ life?

Handout B

Text-Dependent Questions, Text Response, and Personal Reflection

Name: ______________________________

Text-Dependent Questions

1. Concrete nouns can be identified through one or more of the five senses (sight, sound, touch, smell, and taste), such as "swan" and "sugar." Highlight five more concrete nouns.

____

____

2. Action verbs show movement, like "flung" and "floats." Highlight five more action verbs.

____

____

3. In lines 5–6, the poet describes in delicious detail the grasshopper (female) "who has flung herself out of the grass . . . eating sugar out of my hand." Find three more details describing what the grasshopper does and copy them below.

____

____

4. Repetition means repeating something; it's a powerful tool used to emphasize a point in both speaking and writing, as seen in the opening questions: "*Who made* the world?/*Who made* the swan, and the black bear?/*Who made* the grasshopper?" List three more examples of repetition in the poem.

____

____

5. In line 14, the poet proclaims that she knows "how to be *idle* and blessed." What does the word "idle" mean? Use context clues.

____

____

6. Alliteration means repeating the beginning consonant sound in a series of words within a phrase or line, as in "Now she lifts her pale *forearms* and thoroughly washes her *face*" (9). Find one more example in the poem.

____

____

Continued on next page

Text Response

Examine the theme of the poem and its development. Cite textual evidence.

Prompt

At the end of the poem, Oliver asks, "What is it you plan to do/with your one wild and precious life?" (18–19). What is she urging us to do? Include other lines from the poem to support your response.

____

____

____

____

____

____

Self-Reflection

What is the value of stepping away from our screens and connecting with the real world? How are you managing your "digital life"? Give an example.

____

____

____

____

____

____

Handout C

Text-Dependent Questions Answer Key and Sample Text Response

Text-Dependent Questions Answer Key

1. black bear, grasshopper, grass, eyes, forearms, face, fields
2. Flung, eating, moving, gazing, lifts, washes, snaps, floats, fall down, kneel, stroll
3. "moving jaws back and forth instead of up and down"; "gazing around with enormous and complicated eyes"; "thoroughly washes her face"; "snaps her wings open"; "floats away"
4. "the one who . . ."; "now she . . ."; "how to . . ."; "Tell me . . ."
5. "Idle" means still, not moving, not doing anything. "Fall down into the grass, kneel in the grass, stroll through the fields . . ."
6. "black bear"; "what/with/wild"; "plan/precious"

Sample Text Response

In the poem "The Summer Day," Oliver encourages us to slow down so we don't miss the beauty and richness of the present moment before it's gone. In the opening line, she asks the big, cosmic question, "Who made the world?" and in the next one, "Who made the swan, and the black bear?" These questions invite us to consider the wonder that surrounds us. By asking them, she pulls us in and encourages us to reflect upon the purpose of our fleeting lives, which is not only to be busy and productive, but also to be "idle and blessed."

Handout D

Basic Poem Writing Play Sheet

Name: ______________________________

Write your favorite line from the poem:

Next, brainstorm ideas in each of the categories below:

Animals, insects that fascinate	Action verbs: ways they move	Big questions I have

Now use your ideas to write a poem about a pet or other animal or insect you watch closely.

Who made the _________________________?
(animal or insect)

This _________________________, I mean—
(animal or insect)

The one who ____
(What does this animal or insect do?)

Tell me, ____?
(Ask a question.)

Continued on next page

Draw a picture of your animal or insect.

STUDENT EXAMPLE

Who made the chihuahua?
this chihuahua, I mean—
the one who snores beside me on the couch.
Tell me, what do you love?

Handout E

Intermediate Poem Writing Play Sheet

Name: ______________________________

Brainstorm words in the following categories, and then use your ideas to write your own version of the poem.

Animals and insects that fascinate me	What they do (action verbs)	Things I wonder about/big questions	Things that comfort/ground me

Continued on next page

Now use your ideas to write your own version of the poem.

Title: ____

(save this for last and make it surprising or just right for your poem)

Who made the ____________________?
(animal or insect)

This ____________________, I mean—
(animal or insect)

The one who has ____
(action verb as past participle)

The one who is ____
(action)

Who is ____
(action)

I don't know exactly what ________________________ is.
(something I wonder about)

I do know how to ____
(something that grounds me)

How to ____
(something that grounds me)

How to ____
(something that grounds me)

Tell me, ____?
(Ask a big question.)

Tell me, ____?
(Ask a big question.)

Handout F

Advanced Poem Writing Play Sheet

Name: ______________________________

Use the following template as a guide to write your own version of the poem. Feel free to change it or abandon it at any point.

Title: ____

(save this for last and make it surprising or just right for your poem)

Who made the _________________________?

This _________________________, I mean—

The one who has ____

The one who is ____

Who is ____

I don't know exactly what _______________________________ is.

I do know how to ____

How to ____

How to ____

Tell me, ____?

Tell me, ____?

Continued on next page

CREATIVE WRITING EXAMPLES

Poetry

The Rottweiler

Who made the Rottweiler?
This Rottweiler, I mean—
The one who has jumped in the pool,
The one who is tripping over air,
Who is constantly smiling.
I don't know exactly how the sun shines.
I do know how to float on water,
how to spot shapes within the clouds
how to love unconditionally
Tell me, why are you so scared of confrontation?
Tell me, will anyone remember us after we're gone?

—Sammi, eleventh grade

My Ocean

Who made the jellyfish?
This jellyfish, I mean—
The one who has propelled itself through soft currents
The one who is silently alive
Who is flowing wherever the current takes them.
I don't know exactly what power is.
I do know how to listen to my body,
how to take care of my plants,
how to take care of myself.
Tell me, who are you living for?

—Maddy, twelfth grade

REFERENCES, RESOURCES, AND FURTHER READING

Centers for Disease Control and Prevention. "Fast Facts: Preventing Child Abuse & Neglect." www.cdc.gov/violenceprevention/childabuseandneglect/fastfact.html (accessed August 1, 2022).

———. "Fast Facts: Preventing Child Sexual Abuse." www.cdc.gov/violenceprevention/childsexualabuse/fastfact.html (accessed August 1, 2022).

Johnson, Shelli. "'The Summer Day,' by Mary Oliver." Video of poetry reading, 2:16. Uploaded January 22, 2019. www.youtube.com/watch?v=gqaP0m9_vjg (accessed August 1, 2022).

Lesson Three

Belonging to the Natural World

Excerpt, "Song of Myself," Section 2, by Walt Whitman

"Look deep into nature, and then you will understand everything better."

~ Albert Einstein

OBJECTIVES

Mindfulness Skills	Visualize safe place Reflect on interconnectedness with natural world
CASEL Competencies Highlights	Self-awareness: Identify personal, cultural, and linguistic assets; develop interests and a sense of purpose Self-management: Show courage to take initiative; demonstrate personal agency
Creative Writing Task (Aligns with CCSS.ELA-LITERACY.W.9-10.3 a-e; W.9-10.4-6; L.9-10.1 a,b; L.9-10.2 a-c; L.9-10.3 a; ELD Part I, C, 10, 12 and ELD Part II, A-C)	Compose a piece of writing that celebrates one's sense of self
Academic Writing Task (Aligns with CCSS.ELA-LITERACY.W.9-10.1; W.9-10.4-6; L.9-10.1 a, b; L.9-10.2 a-c; L.9-10.3 a; ELD Part I, C, 11, 12 and ELD Part II, A-C)	Analyze theme and its development in poem

INTRODUCTION

In his celebratory masterpiece, "Song of Myself," Walt Whitman breathes in all the sights and sounds of the world around him and breathes out poetry. He invites us to fully inhabit our bodies and cue into our breath and our senses. Young people will perk up their ears at "a few light kisses, a few embraces, a reaching around of arms." For Whitman, poetry is organic, visceral, and not the intellectual endeavor to which it can sometimes be reduced. The poem's revolutionary message is to stop and exercise one's ability "to listen to all sides and filter them from your self." The clear seeing that results from distilling what we hear from others (and what we tell ourselves) is the gift of mindfulness.

DID YOU KNOW? NATURALIST INTELLIGENCE

In 2006, twenty-three years after developing his theory of multiple types of intelligence, Howard Gardner added an eighth branch: *naturalist intelligence*, or "nature smart." This ability to recognize plants, animals, and other elements of the natural world helped our ancestors distinguish between edible and poisonous mushrooms, harmless and potentially deadly snakes, predators, and a myriad of other distinctions vital to their survival.

People with a strong naturalist intelligence demonstrate a keen awareness of and concern for the environment, so important given the climate challenges we are currently facing. For teachers in rural settings, and those working with English learners, many who come from still largely agrarian societies, highlighting "nature smarts" provides an excellent opportunity to recognize and honor the knowledge and skills these students bring to the classroom. Not surprisingly, research suggests that connecting with nature, whether it be in one's own backyard, a neighborhood park, or a community garden, reduces stress and promotes well-being.

STUDENT LESSON OBJECTIVES

- ✔ Create an image in your mind of a safe place
- ✔ Think about your relationship with nature and how it can support you
- ✔ Reflect on your strengths and ways to develop greater self-confidence
- ✔ Do a close reading of an excerpt from the poem "Song of Myself" by Walt Whitman and answer questions about it
- ✔ Write your own version of the poem or a story inspired by it
- ✔ Write a paragraph sharing what you think the poet's message is and find lines from the poem to support your ideas

Step 1: Quick Write (5 min.) and Partner Share (5 min.)

Prompt: Write about a time you when you became so totally absorbed in something that you lost track of time. It could have been due to watching a sunset or a bee hunting for pollen, or sitting on the floor of your bedroom closet, making your own magic.

Step 2: Guided Mindfulness Practice (5–7 min.)

Teacher Note: The following practice invites students to imagine themselves in a safe place, where they can take off their masks and simply be themselves. This place could be outside, resting in the loving embrace of the nonjudgmental natural world. You might like to discuss nature as a resource and support for them—a tree won't lend you money, but it won't judge or criticize you, either. If nature doesn't work for a student, they can visualize themselves in their bedroom, or another place they visit only in their imagination.

Script

When we receive text messages from our friends, we may feel happy. And as you may have also experienced, sometimes people say things in the heat of the moment they wish they hadn't said. Creating a safe place within yourself can be helpful at these times. It's a place you can visit in your imagination whenever you want or need to.

Let's begin by arriving fully into this moment . . . allowing whatever has happened so far today to melt away . . . coming back to the body. Scan for any areas of tension—maybe in the shoulders, the neck (demonstrate movements) *. . . Roll the shoulders back and down and* *move the head from side to side, dropping the chin to the chest and interlacing the fingers behind the head to gently deepen the stretch. Then on the inhale, look up to the ceiling and stretch through the chest. Take a few deep breaths, inviting the breath to reach into the belly, then expanding it like a balloon and finally sighing it out through the mouth on the exhale.*

Now bring your full attention to the sound of the bell. (Ring bell.)

Rest your elbows on your desk and place your forehead in the palms of your hands. Notice any sensations—maybe warmth, vibration, pulsing. . . . (Pause.) *And if you feel comfortable, allow your eyes to close and imagine in your mind's eye a beautiful place that's special to you. It could be a place you've been before or one that you create in your imagination—beside a river or near the ocean, on a star or planet far away . . . or in your own backyard. And if your image is a bit hazy or unclear, that's okay, too . . . just do the best you can. Take in the environment and notice what you see around you* (pause), *what you hear* (pause). *Find a comfortable place to lie down and rest for a while and just be . . .* (pause), *no need to do anything or be anyone.* (Ring bell.)

Step 3: Debrief (partners, then whole class, 5–10 min.)

1. What did you notice?
2. Where was your safe place? What did you see there? Hear? Smell? Taste? Touch?
3. How do you feel now?

Step 4: Read Excerpt from "Song of Myself" (2 min.)

Read poem aloud. Encourage students to visualize what they hear.

Step 5: Making Connections (5–10 min.)

1. What do you like about the poem? What images stand out in your mind?
2. What words or phrases do you remember?
3. What is the poem saying to you?

Step 6: Cloze Listening Activity (Handout A) (10 min.)

Ask students to sort the vocabulary words by parts of speech. Then read the poem aloud a second time, pausing while students fill in the missing words.

Step 7: Text-Dependent Questions (Handout B; Answers on Handout C) (15–20 min.)

Distribute Handout B for students to complete questions, either alone, with a partner, or in small groups.

Step 8: Text Response (Handout B; Sample Response on Handout C)

Prompt: Why do you think Whitman titled his poem "The Song of Myself"? What is he encouraging us to do?

Step 9: Self-Reflection (Handout B)

Prompt: What brings you joy? How do you celebrate being you?

Step 10: Poem Writing

Brainstorm (10–15 min.)

Post sheets of paper around classroom with the following categories written on them and have students write one idea on each:

- pairs of opposite words to describe breathing (i.e., expanding/contracting, rising/falling, coming/going)
- sights, sounds, and smells of the natural world
- things for which we are grateful
- things we are good at doing/our accomplishments
- amazing things we can't buy (no matter how much money we have)
- habits we'd like to change
- advice we'd like to give ourselves

Poem Writing (Handout D, E, or F) (10–15 min.)

Distribute Handout D, E, or F, depending on students' fluency in English and creative writing experience.

Step 11: Prose Writing Options

1. ***Prompt:*** Expand upon the ideas generated in the quick write about a time when you became totally absorbed in something. Describe the scene using as much detail as possible. What thoughts, feelings, and sensations arose for you? What did you learn about yourself through this experience?
2. ***Prompt:*** Draw and write about the safe place created in your mind during the guided visualization.

TAKEAWAY

A tree does not stand in self-judgment, wishing it could do something about its branches and leaves. Whitman eloquently reminds us of our deep connection to nature and its accepting and healing powers.

EXTENSION

This excerpt from "Song of Myself" may be paired with a mindful nature walk, inviting students to touch the earth, hug trees, and smell the flowers. If there's a school garden, students might taste mint leaves, crush lavender flowers beneath their fingertips, and peer into hibiscus blossoms. This walk could serve to orient new students to the campus and have the fringe benefit of making you seem like one of the most "savage" teachers there.

To awaken the senses and inspire creative output without leaving the classroom, students could experience a range of fresh herbs, essential oils, or a single rose. Collecting items for a sensory box, such as a rain stick, colored feathers, rocks and pinecones, an emery board, and squishy toys, provides students with a smorgasbord of sensory delights (and calmed nerves).

From "Song of Myself," Section 2
by Walt Whitman

The smoke of my own breath,
Echoes, ripples, buzz'd whispers, love-root, silk-thread, crotch and vine,
My respiration and inspiration, the beating of my heart, the passing of blood and air through my lungs,
5 The sniff of green leaves and dry leaves, and of the shore and dark-color'd sea-rocks, and of the hay in the barn,
The sound of the belch'd words of my voice loos'd to the eddies of the wind,
A few light kisses, a few embraces, a reaching around of arms,
The play of shine and shade on the trees as the supple boughs wag,
10 The delight alone or in the rush of the streets, or along the fields and hill-sides,
The feeling of health, the full-noon trill, the song of me rising from bed and meeting the sun.

Have you reckon'd a thousand acres much? have you reckon'd the earth much?
Have you practis'd so long to learn to read?
15 Have you felt so proud to get at the meaning of poems?

Stop this day and night with me and you shall possess the origin of all poems,
You shall possess the good of the earth and sun, (there are millions of suns left,)
You shall no longer take things at second or third hand, nor look through the eyes of the dead, nor feed on the specters in books,
20 You shall not look through my eyes either, nor take things from me,
You shall listen to all sides and filter them from your self.

Handout A

Cloze Listening Activity

Name: ______________________________

Sort the missing words into parts of speech.

acres	barn	beating	blood	breath	buzz'd	
delight	dry	feed on	filter	full-noon	kisses	meaning
meeting	millions	possess	read	shore		
sound	supple	vine	wind			

Adjectives	Nouns	Verbs
full-noon	delight	filter

Continued on next page

Now listen to the poem and use the words to fill in the blanks.

From "Song of Myself," Section 2
by Walt Whitman

The smoke of my own (1) ____________,
Echoes, ripples, (2) ____________ whispers, love-root, silk-thread, crotch and
(3) ____________,
My respiration and inspiration, the (4) ____________ of my heart, the passing of
(5) ____________ and air through my lungs,
5 The sniff of green leaves and (6) ____________ leaves, and of the (7) ____________
and dark-color'd sea-rocks,
and of the hay in the (8) ____________,
The (9) ____________ of the belch'd words of my voice loos'd to the eddies of the
(10) ____________,
A few light (11) ____________, a few embraces, a reaching around of arms,
The play of shine and shade on the trees as the (12) ____________ boughs wag,
10 The (13) ____________ alone or in the rush of the streets, or along the fields and hill-sides,
The feeling of health, the (14) ____________ trill, the song of me rising from bed and
(15) ____________ the sun.

Have you reckon'd a thousand (16) ____________ much? have you reckon'd the earth much?
Have you practis'd so long to learn to (17) ____________?
15 Have you felt so proud to get at the (18) ____________ of poems?

Stop this day and night with me and you shall (19) ____________ the origin of all poems,
You shall possess the good of the earth and sun, (there are (20) ____________ of suns left,)
You shall no longer take things at second or third-hand, nor look through the eyes of
the dead, nor (21) ____________ the specters in books,
20 You shall not look through my eyes either, nor take things from me,
You shall listen to all sides and (22) ____________ them from your self.

Handout B

Text-Dependent Questions, Text Response, and Personal Reflection

Name: ______________________________

Text-Dependent Questions

1. The first stanza (1–12) of the poem consists of a playful and elegant list, which shows the poet's deep connection with the natural world, almost transcending the boundaries of his physical body. For example, in line 2, he writes, "Echoes, ripples, buzz'd whispers, love-root, silk-thread, crotch and vine." Highlight three of your favorite phrases in this first part of the poem.

____

____

2. The first line, "The smoke of my own breath," shows the poet's appreciation for being alive. Find three more phrases that celebrate being alive and/or, most probably, in love.

____

____

3. In the second part of the excerpt (13–21), Whitman speaks directly to us, his readers. What effect does this direct address have?

____

____

4. In this second part, Whitman pokes fun at those who might feel they have mastered the art of letter and of interpreting poetry. What questions does he ask us? (Cite textual evidence.)

____

____

5. In line 18, the poet encourages us to trust ourselves—"You shall no longer take things at second or third-hand." Find another line that demonstrates this call to courage and self-confidence. (Cite textual evidence.)
6. What does it mean to "listen to all sides and filter them from your self"? (21).

____

____

Continued on next page

HANDOUT B 2 / 2

Text Response

Examine the theme of the poem and its development. Cite textual evidence.

Prompt

Why do you think Whitman titled his poem "Song of Myself"? What is he encouraging us to do?

____

____

____

____

Self-Reflection

What brings you joy? How do you celebrate being you?

____

____

____

____

Handout C

Text-Dependent Questions Answer Key and Sample Text Response

Text-Dependent Questions Answer Key

1. *Answers will vary.*
2. my respiration and inspiration, the beating of my heart, the passing of blood and air through my lungs, buzz'd whispers, love-root, crotch, a few light kisses, a few embraces, a reaching around of arms
3. The reader is called to listen more closely.
4. "Have you practis'd so long to learn to read?/Have you felt so proud to get at the meaning of poems?"
5. "Nor look through the eyes of the dead, nor feed on the specters in books. You shall not look through my eyes either, nor take things from me,/You shall listen to all sides and filter them from your self."
6. Come to your own conclusion based on your analysis of what others have said.

Sample Text Response

Whitman titled his poem "Song of Myself" because it is a celebration of living life with awareness. By learning to listen to the wisdom of the body, as well as trusting our own intuition, we develop greater clarity, confidence, and strength to remain true to ourselves. In line 16, he invites us: "Stop this day and night with me and you shall possess the origin of all poems. . . . You shall no longer take things at second or third hand, nor look through the eyes of the dead, nor feed on the specters in books." As a gay poet in the early nineteenth century, Whitman might have also been giving himself advice on how to lead an authentic life.

Handout D

Basic Poem Writing Play Sheet

Name: ______________________________

Write your favorite line from the excerpt from "Song of Myself" below:

____

Next, add three to five nouns to each category to add details to your poem.

Special Places	See	Feel	Listen To	Like To (action verbs)

Continued on next page

Next, complete the sentences:

My special place is ____

I like to see ______________________, to feel ______________________,

and to listen to ____.

Sometimes I ____.
(What do you do there?)

That's why I love to be in ____.
(your special place)

Handout E

Intermediate Poem Writing Play Sheet

Name: ______________________________

Directions: Brainstorm words in the following categories, and then use your ideas to write your own version of the poem.

Title: ____

(save the title for last and make it surprising or just right for your words)

The smoke of my breath

____

(pair of opposite words to describe breathing—i.e., rising/falling, expanding/contracting, coming/going, arriving/departing)

Myself, ____

(something majestic and beautiful from nature)

The sniff of ____________________________________

(something you smell)

The sound of ____________________________________

(something you hear)

Have you reckon'd how lucky you are to ____________________________________?

(something you're grateful for)

Have you practiced so long to learn to ____________________________________?

(a skill you possess)

Have you felt so proud to ____________________________________?

(an accomplishment)

Stop this day and night with me and you shall possess ____________________________________

(something amazing you can't buy)

You shall no longer ____________________________________

(a habit you'd like to break)

You shall ____

(a piece of advice you'd like to give yourself)

Handout F

Advanced Poem Writing Play Sheet

Name: ______________________________

Use the following template as a guide to write your own version of the poem. Feel free to change it or abandon it at any point.

Title: ____
(save the title for last and make it surprising or just right for your words)

The smoke of my breath

____

Myself, ____

The sniff of ____

The sound of ____

Have you reckon'd how lucky you are to ___________________________________?

Have you practiced so long to learn to ___________________________________?

Have you felt so proud to ___________________________________?

Stop this day and night with me and you shall possess ________________________________

You shall no longer ___________________________________

You shall ___________________________________

CREATIVE WRITING EXAMPLES

Poetry

The smoke of my breath
Breathe in/breathe out
Chest rising, calming,
A blue sky, an ocean
Myself, a bird in a beautiful day
The sniff of my friends' perfume when we hug each other
The sound of our kisses

Have you reckon'd how lucky you are to have people around you that love you?
Have you practiced so long to learn to love the people that love you?
Have you felt so proud to have beautiful people around you?

Stop this day and night with me and you shall possess a peaceful life.
You shall no longer fight in school.
You shall be nice to other people.

—Maria S., seventh grade, English learner

Prose

My Natural History

My story is brought to a place where you feel the life of other natural things. The mountain is a very special place for me. I like to see the pine trees, feel the wind move them, and listen to the noise they make. I like to hear the song of the birds. Sometimes I see deer and that's why I love to be alone in nature.

—Andrea, tenth grade, English learner

REFERENCES, RESOURCES, AND FURTHER READING

Capaldi, Colin A., Holli-Anne Passmore, Elizabeth K. Nisbet, John M. Zelenski, Raelyne L. Dopko. "Flourishing in Nature: A Review of the Benefits of Connecting with Nature and Its Application as a Wellbeing Intervention." *International Journal of Wellbeing.* 5, no. 4 (December 2015): 1–16.

Louv, Richard. *Last Child in the Woods*. New York: Algonquin Books, 2008.

Sadiku, Matthew N. O., Tolulope J. Ashaolu, and Sarhan M. Musa. "Naturalistic Intelligence." *International Journal of Scientific Advances* 1, no. 1 (July–August 2020). www.ijscia.com/wp-content/uploads/2020/07/Volume1-Issue-1-Jul-Aug-2020-No.1-1-4.pdf.

Whitman, Walt. "Song of Myself: 2." *Why Poetry Matters*. Video montage and poetry reading, 2:11. Uploaded May 6, 2011. www.youtube.com/watch?v=GX7ssynVkg4 (accessed August 1, 2022).

Lesson Four

Why Practice Mindfulness?

"Keeping Quiet" by Pablo Neruda

> *"All of humanity's problems stem from man's inability to sit quietly in a room alone."*
>
> *~ Blaise Pascal*

OBJECTIVES

Mindfulness Skills	Describe what mindfulness means and how it relates to wellness Experiment using the breath as an anchor of attention Cultivate curiosity and kind, nonjudgmental awareness of thoughts, feelings, and bodily sensations
CASEL Competencies Highlights	Self-awareness: Identify one's thoughts and emotions Self-management: Identify and use stress-management techniques
Creative Writing Task (Aligns with CCSS.ELA-LITERACY.W.9-10.3 a-e; W.9-10.4-6; L.9-10.1 a,b; L.9-10.2 a-c; L.9-10.3 a; ELD Part I, C, 10, 12 and ELD Part II, A-C)	Create a poem or personal narrative that celebrates a moment of presence
Academic Writing Task (Aligns with CCSS.ELA-LITERACY.W.9-10.1; W.9-10.4-6; L.9-10.1 a, b; L.9-10.2 a-c; L.9-10.3 a; ELD Part I, C, 11, 12 and ELD Part II, A-C)	Analyze theme and its development in poem

INTRODUCTION

Another word for mindfulness is awareness. Cultivating awareness of our thoughts, feelings, and body sensations, and seeing how all these phenomena arise and pass away like clouds in the sky, is to begin to see the truth of our experiences—namely, that nothing is permanent. What pops up in our consciousness does not define us. This is good news, given the fear, judgment, and anger of which we inevitably become aware as we practice "keeping quiet." Rather than experiencing serenity, we may find ourselves preparing "green wars, wars with gas, wars with fire." This is the nature of the untrained mind. The beauty of the practice is that it addresses our deepest longings as human beings: to attain emotional maturity and dedicate our lives to something larger than ourselves.

DID YOU KNOW? CURIOSITY AND ACADEMIC SUCCESS

Along with intelligence and effort, researchers rank curiosity as one of the three most important predictors of academic success. The etymology of the word "school" comes from the ancient Greek *schole*, which refers to a mode of learning including contemplation, conversation, and poetic ways of knowing, rather than rational thought and analysis alone. Returning to a "slow school" model, a "School of Wonder," which cultivates students' authentic desire to know based on *their* interests and their innate longing to understand themselves, can reenergize the school climate. Doing so as part of a supportive community that encourages risk-taking and normalizes fear and anxiety can lead to powerful results.

Curiosity also promotes students' well-being. A study conducted with over four hundred teens in Serbia found that the more curious youth tended to be optimistic and purposeful as well as more kind and accepting of themselves in the face of life's unpredictability.

STUDENT LESSON OBJECTIVES

- ✔ Describe what mindfulness is and how it can benefit you
- ✔ Practice counting your breaths to focus your attention
- ✔ Be open and kind to whatever thoughts, feelings, and bodily sensations you notice
- ✔ Write your own version of "Keeping Quiet" or a story inspired by it
- ✔ Write a paragraph sharing what you think the poet's message is and include some lines from the poem to show your understanding

Step 1: Quick Write (5 min.) and Partner Share (5 min.)

Prompt: Describe an activity you enjoy doing to help you relax. When do you do it? Do you do it alone or with others? How do you feel afterward?

Step 2: Guided Practice (5–7 min.)

Teacher Note: This guided practice introduces breath as an anchor of attention. Having students count their breaths gives them a simple technique for developing their focus and concentration. If students don't feel comfortable using their breath, they may focus on sounds, body sensations, or colors and shapes in their environment.

Script

Take a rest. Roll your shoulders down and back a few times. Then roll them forward a few times . . . moving your head from side to side, dropping your chin to the chest and gently rolling it to one shoulder and then the other. (Pause.) *Let go of any tension in the face—behind the eyes, in the forehead . . . opening and closing the mouth, moving the jaw from side to side to release any holding.*

Listen to the bell. (Ring bell.) *Then invite stillness into your body, noticing the support of the chair and the floor beneath you. There is no place to go. Nothing to do. No one to be. Breathe in deeply, allowing your belly to rise, and then exhaling. Touch into the natural rhythm of the breath.* (Pause.) *Now notice your breath at the nostrils . . . feel the coolness of the breath on the inhale, and the slight warmth of the breath on the exhale.* (Pause.) *Play with narrowing your attention to this one object. If it feels comfortable, experiment with counting your breaths. On the exhale, gently say to yourself "one," and continue to count your breaths, one exhale at a time. You may choose to count five or ten breaths, and if you lose track, no problem. That's a moment of mindfulness.* (Pause for 1–2 minutes.)

Notice what it feels like to keep quiet. Maybe it feels strange or uncomfortable. Bring awareness to what thoughts and emotions come up for you . . . none is right or wrong. We're cultivating curiosity about our inner experiences, and it's not something we normally do, so if you feel like laughing or blowing it off, just notice that and see if you can bring yourself back to the experiment of counting your breaths. . . . (Pause.)

The practice of mindfulness is just being with whatever is arising, accepting it as it is, and knowing that it will change. Whatever you notice is okay. Just bring your curiosity to this moment and this breath. (Pause, and then invite a student to ring the bell.)

Step 3: Debrief Counting Breaths (partners, then whole class, 5–10 min.)

1. Were you able to count your breaths? How did it feel?
2. Did you return to the number "one" when you got distracted? Were you kind to yourself if this took place?
3. What else did you notice?

Step 4: Read "Keeping Quiet" (2 min.)

Read poem aloud. Encourage students to visualize what they hear.

Step 5: Making Connections (5–10 min.)

1. What do you appreciate about this poem?
2. What words or phrases do you remember?
3. What images stand out in your mind?

Step 6: Cloze Listening Worksheet (Handout A) (10 min.)

Discuss new vocabulary words. Then read the poem aloud a second time or have a student volunteer do so, pausing while students fill in the missing words.

Step 7: Text-Dependent Questions (Handout B; Answers on Handout C) (15–20 min.)

Distribute Handout B for students to complete questions, either alone, with a partner, or in small groups.

Step 8: Text Response (Handout B; Sample Response on Handout C)

Prompt: Why does Neruda encourage us to "keep quiet"? How can doing so help us be better social beings and reduce harm in the world?

Step 9: Self-Reflection (Handout B)

Prompt: How can practicing mindfulness help you to understand yourself better?

Step 10: Poem Writing (Handout D, E, or F) (10–15 min.)

Distribute Handout D, E, or F, depending on students' fluency in English and creative writing experience.

Step 11: Prose Writing Option

Prompt: Write about a time when you stopped yourself and did nothing instead of causing yourself or someone else harm.

TAKEAWAY

Practicing pausing is moving upstream from the frenetic currents of our modern society flowing in the opposite direction. While the journey may take a lifetime, it's *a journey of a lifetime*.

EXTENSION

For exhausted teenagers who may find their breath too subtle to focus their attention on, you may like to explore the practice of the body scan. A student favorite, the body scan invites them to bring their awareness to sensations in their bodies—warmth or coolness, heaviness or lightness, tingling, pulsing, throbbing, or perhaps, numbness—and any emotions that may arise. The intention is to build the capacity to simply observe one's experience without grasping, judging, or rejecting it. This practice is traditionally done while lying down, and a full body scan can easily last between twenty and forty-five minutes. This abbreviated version lasts between seven and ten minutes, and it could be revisited later in the course for a longer period of time.

Script

Practicing mindfulness trains us to feel safer and more comfortable in our own skin. In this practice, we're going to bring a flashlight of attention to different parts of our bodies, beginning with the feet and moving to the head, inviting relaxation and awareness into each part. If your mind wanders or you notice judgments arise, that's okay. That's a moment of awareness and a great time to offer yourself compassion. You might like to imagine this light as a warm globe, bringing love and acceptance to your body and mind.

(Demonstrate the following movements.) *So, find a comfortable position with both feet flat on the floor. Your back should be upright, shoulders back and down, head and neck relaxed. You might like to roll your shoulders back a few times and move your head from side to side; then loosen your jaw. Now rest your eyes in their sockets, and if you feel comfortable doing so, gently close your eyes or lower them and soften your gaze. I'll ring the bell three times and invite you to bring your full attention to the sound, as a reminder to bring yourself home to your body.* (Ring bell.)

Now notice your whole body seated in space . . . feel the weight of your feet connecting with the floor and the pressure of your legs and back against the chair. Find the breath in your belly, and enjoy a few deep breaths, inhaling new life and exhaling the old. (Pause for a few breaths.) *And then, breathe normally.*

Now bring the light of awareness on the inhale to your feet. Just for a moment, notice the life of your feet. You may be aware of tingling or vibrating in your toes, your arches, the outsides of your feet, and your heels. Feel the sensations—pulsing, maybe aching or throbbing—and notice the temperature, whether heat or coolness. Allow the feet to be just as they are. (Pause.) *And then, release your feet on the exhale.* (Pause.)

Now return with your awareness and your breath back to the belly. If you like, you might place your hands on your belly, noticing the rise and fall with your breath and what's alive for you here—perhaps a feeling of fullness or hunger. This is an area of the body where strong emotions, like anxiety, worry, fear, or shame, may be stored. If so, that's okay. Just acknowledge what's present, and with your awareness, breathe in relaxation and ease with a warm, loving light; then exhale all that does not serve you. (Pause.)

Now move into the chest. Place a hand there if you like and notice the expansion on the inhale and the contraction on the exhale. (Pause.) *What's alive for you here? Maybe lightness or heaviness. Notice any emotions that may be present. This is an area where many people feel sadness and grief, and they may notice a contracted sensation around the heart. If this is true for you, no judgment. Once again, imagine the light of loving awareness softening this area with your breath, inviting acceptance and ease.* (Pause.)

Now release this area with the exhale and move into your head. Notice your skull, your jaw. When we concentrate, we tend to tighten the forehead, so consciously relax through this area and release all the muscles of your face. Imagine your face being made of wax, and the mask beginning to melt away in a warm, loving light. (Pause.) *Feel the flow of sensation, whether subtle or strong, and let life be just as it is.*

Now bring awareness to your whole body and scan for any areas of tension that may remain. (Pause.) *Soften and release them with the exhale.* (Pause.) *And as you feel ready, take another deep inhalation, and begin to wiggle your fingers and toes and gently open your eyes.* (Ring bell.)

Debrief

1. What did you notice?
2. What parts of your body were easy to connect with? Difficult to connect with?
3. What sensations, emotions, thoughts, and judgments arose?

Keeping Quiet
by Pablo Neruda

Now we will count to twelve
and we will all keep still.
For once on the face of the earth,
let's not speak in any language;
5 let's stop for one second,
and not move our arms so much.
It would be an exotic moment
without rush, without engines;
we would all be together
10 in a sudden strangeness.
Fishermen in the cold sea
would not harm whales
and the man gathering salt
would not look at his hurt hands.
15 Those who prepare green wars,
wars with gas, wars with fire,
victories with no survivors,
would put on clean clothes
and walk about with their brothers
20 in the shade, doing nothing.
What I want should not be confused
with total inactivity.
Life is what it is about;
I want no truck with death.
25 If we were not so single-minded
about keeping our lives moving,
and for once could do nothing,
perhaps a huge silence
might interrupt this sadness
30 of never understanding ourselves
and of threatening ourselves with death.
Perhaps the earth can teach us
as when everything seems dead
and later proves to be alive.
35 Now I'll count up to twelve
and you keep quiet and I will go.

Handout A

Cloze Listening Activity

Name: ______________________________

Sort the words below into parts of speech.

alive	arms	death	exotic	fishermen	green	hands
inactivity	interrupt	nothing	perhaps	proves	quiet	single-minded
speak	still	strangeness	survivors	twelve	understanding	whales

Adjective	Noun	Verb
alive	arms	interrupt

Continued on next page

Now listen to the poem and use the words to fill in the blanks.

Keeping Quiet
by Pablo Neruda

Now we will count to (1) ______________
and we will all keep (2) ______________.
For once on the face of the earth,
let's not (3) ______________ in any language;
5 let's stop for one second,
and not move our (4) ______________ so much.
It would be an (5) ______________ moment
without rush, without engines;
we would all be together
10 in a sudden (6) ______________.
(7) ______________ in the cold sea
would not harm (8) ______________
and the man gathering salt
would not look at his hurt (9) ______________.
15 Those who prepare (10) ______________ wars,
wars with gas, wars with fire,
victories with no (11) ______________,
would put on clean clothes
and walk about with their brothers
20 in the shade, doing (12) ______________.
What I want should not be confused
with total (13) ______________.
Life is what it is about;
I want no truck with death.
25 If we were not so (14) ______________
about keeping our lives moving,
and for once could do nothing,

Continued on next page

perhaps a huge silence
might (15) _______________ this sadness
30 of never (16) _______________ ourselves
and of threatening ourselves with (17) _______________.
(18) _______________ the earth can teach us
as when everything seems dead
and later (19) _______________ to be alive.
35 Now I'll count up to twelve
and you keep (20) _______________ and I will go.

Handout B

Text-Dependent Questions, Text Response, and Personal Reflection

Name: ______________________

Text-Dependent Questions

1. Circle or highlight ten concrete nouns in the poem. What images pop up in your mind?

____

____

2. In lines 3–4, the poet writes, "For once on the face of the earth, let's not speak in any language." To whom is he talking?

____

____

3. In lines 5–6, Neruda writes, "Let's stop for one second/and not move our arms so much." What two definitions, or meanings, does the word "arms" have?

____

____

4. Wars happen both inside ourselves (internally) and in the world (externally). What lines refer to the inner war?

____

____

5. Repetition creates rhythm and cohesiveness. One example is "Let's not speak . . . /Let's stop." Find two other examples of repetition in the poem.

____

____

6. Alliteration is repeating the beginning consonant, as in "sudden strangeness." Find three other examples in the poem.

____

____

Continued on next page

Text Response

Examine the theme and its development in the poem.

Prompt

Why does Neruda encourage us to "keep quiet"? How can doing so help us be better social beings or reduce harm in the world? Cite textual evidence.

____

____

____

____

____

____

Self-Reflection

How can practicing mindfulness help you to understand yourself better? Give an example from your life.

____

____

____

____

____

____

Handout C

Text-Dependent Questions Answer Key and Sample Text Response

Text-Dependent Questions Answer Key

1. arms, engines, fishermen, sea, whales, salt, man, hands, gas, fire, clothes; along the seashore
2. all peoples in all places, speaking all languages
3. body part, weapon
4. "this sadness of never understanding ourselves/and of threatening ourselves with death"
5. "without rush, without engines"; "fishermen . . . would not/ the man . . . would not"; "green wars, wars with gas, wars with fire"
6. hurt hands, clean clothes, silence/sadness

Sample Text Response

In the poem "Keeping Quiet," Neruda encourages us to practice self-reflection so we may experience greater serenity and self-knowledge. He also suggests that by doing so, we may contribute to a more peaceful world. Toward the end of the poem, in lines 25–31, he states, "If we were not so single-minded/about keeping our lives moving,/and for once could do nothing,/perhaps a huge silence/might interrupt this sadness/of never understanding ourselves/and of threatening ourselves with death." These lines refer to the pain and suffering that result from living a superficial, materialistic life in which pausing to know ourselves intimately is not prioritized.

HANDOUT D

Handout D

Basic Poem Writing Play Sheet

Name: ______________________________

Directions: Draw a picture of yourself when you're relaxed. Where are you? Are you alone, or is someone else with you? What are you doing? How do you feel?

When I'm at peace doing nothing, I'm ______________________________________
(Where are you?)

drinking ___________________ and looking at ___________________.
(favorite beverage) *(What do you see?)*

I feel ___________________ and ___________________.
(emotion) *(emotion)*

Handout E

Intermediate Poem Writing Play Sheet

Name: ______________________________

Brainstorm words in the following categories, and then use your ideas to write your own version of the first half of the poem.

Groups of people at work or play	Place where they do activity	Animals/ insects	Parts of the body	Pleasurable activities

Continued on next page

HANDOUT E 2 / 2

Title: ____
(save the title for last and make it surprising or just right for your words)

Now we will count to _______________
(number)

and we will all keep still.

It would be a _______________ moment.
(adjective)

without _______________, without _______________.
(noun) *(noun)*

_______________ in the _______________ _______________
(group of people) *(adjective)* *(place)*

would not harm ______________________________
(animal or persons)

and the _______________ _______________ _______________
(person or group) *(action verb with –ing)* *(object)*

would not look at _______________ _______________ _______________.
(pronoun) *(adjective)* *(body part)*

__________ would _______________ with __________ _______________
(pron.) *(pleasurable activity)* *(pron.)* *(object)*

and _______________ with _______________
(pleasurable activity) *(person, animal)*

in the _______________, doing nothing.
(place)

Handout F

Advanced Poem Writing Play Sheet

Name: ______________________________

Use the following template as a guide to write your own version of the poem. Feel free to change it or abandon it at any point.

Title: ____

(save the title for last and make it surprising or just right for your words)

Now we will count to __________________

And we will all keep still.

It would be a __________________ moment.

Without __________________, without __________________.

__________________ in the __________________ __________________

would not harm ____________________________________

and the __________________ __________________ __________________

would not look at ____________________________________

She/He/They would____________________________________ __________________

and __________________ with __________________

____________________________________ doing nothing.

CREATIVE WRITING EXAMPLES

Poetry

Now we will count to 15
and we will all keep still.
It would be a calm moment
without phones, without devices.
Friends talking in the park
would not harm the weak
and the athlete running with the soccer ball
would not look at his hand.
He would lie down with his soccer ball
and chat with his teammate
in the grass, doing nothing.

—Tristan, ninth grade

Now we will count to 78
and we will all keep still.
It would be a fantastic moment.
without stress, without depression.
Friends at the beach
would not harm seagulls
and the girls taking selfies
would not feel their broken hearts.
They would have a picnic with watermelon
and relax with each other
on the sand, doing nothing.

—Andrea, tenth grade, English learner

Prose

Walk Away

It was Friday the 13th, and I was on my way home when this kid called me the B word. My friends said, “Hey, he’s talking crap about you!”

“Like what? I asked.

“He’s talking about your mom.”

I said to myself, *You know, what’s the point of fighting if you can just talk it out?*

I went up to him and said, “Hey Alex, what’s your problem with me?”

“You keep talking smack about me.”

“No, I wasn’t!”

"Yes, you were!"

"When?" I asked.

"During lunch."

"So, you're mad because people say that I called you something? If I was going to say something to you, I would have said it to your face."

When we finished talking, he said, "So, are you going to fight or not?"

"No," I said. But even though I said no, he still hit me. Everyone screamed, "Fight! Fight!" like six times. I asked myself, *Should I fight him, yes or no?*

I breathed in and out. I said, "You know what? I am not going to fight you."

I went home. Mindfulness.

—Luis, seventh grade, English learner

REFERENCES, RESOURCES, AND FURTHER READING

Eva, Amy. "How to Cultivate Curiosity in Your Classroom." https://greatergood.berkeley.edu/article/item/how_to_cultivate_curiosity_in_your_classroom (accessed August 1, 2022).

Jovanovic, Veljko, and Brdaric Dragana. "Did Curiosity Kill the Cat? Evidence from Subjective Well-Being in Adolescents." *Personality and Individual Differences* 52, no. 3 (February 2012): 380–84.

Keator, Mary. *Lectio Divina as Contemplative Pedagogy: Re-appropriating Monastic Practice for the Humanities.* New York: Routledge, 2017.

Mindfulness Exercises. "Compassionate Body Scan—a Guided Meditation by Kristin Neff." YouTube video, 24:00. July 9, 2020. www.youtube.com/watch?v=FOm6dhob_tw (accessed August 1, 2022).

Neruda, Pablo. "Keeping Quiet." Directed by illneas. Video montage and poetry reading, 3:57. Uploaded June 12, 2020. www.youtube.com/watch?v=k5kjfqbt-FA (accessed August 1, 2022).

Stumm, Sophie von, Benedikt Hell, Tomas Chamorro-Premuzic. "The Hungry Mind: Intellectual Curiosity Is the Third Pillar of Academic Performance." *Perspectives on Psychological Sciences* (October 2011): 574–88.

Lesson Five

Self-Compassion

"Kindness" by Naomi Shihab Nye

> *"Self-knowledge is the beginning of wisdom, which is the ending of fear."*
>
> *~ Jiddu Krishnamurti*

OBJECTIVES

Mindfulness Skills	Familiarize oneself with the physical manifestations of emotions in the body and practice self-compassion
CASEL Competencies Highlight	Self-management: Manage emotions, identify and use stress-management techniques
Creative Writing Task (Aligns with CCSS.ELA-LITERACY.W.9-10.3 a-e; W.9-10.4-6; L.9-10.1 a,b; L.9-10.2 a-c; L.9-10.3 a; ELD Part I, C, 10, 12 and ELD Part II, A-C)	Produce a poem or personal narrative reflecting upon loss
Academic Writing Task (Aligns with CCSS.ELA-LITERACY.W.9-10.1; W.9-10.4-6; L.9-10.1 a, b; L.9-10.2 a-c; L.9-10.3 a; ELD Part I, C, 11, 12 and ELD Part II, A-C)	Analyze theme and its development in poem

INTRODUCTION

The poem "Kindness" can awaken empathy and compassion in the heart of even the most self-protected teen. We've all experienced sadness, disappointment, and loss, and acknowledging our shared humanity and vulnerability builds authentic community. Taking the lead by giving an example from our own lives helps to create safety and encourages others to share. These stories should come "from scars and not wounds"—experiences on which we have gained some perspective and from which we can pull meaning, says Catherine Burns, artistic director of The Moth, an internationally acclaimed nonprofit dedicated to the art and craft of storytelling.

DID YOU KNOW? THE SCIENCE OF SELF-COMPASSION

The poem "Kindness" provides good medicine to those who may be feeling hollow or frozen inside. At the end of the poem, like a warm hug or a caress, Kindness declares, "It is I you have been looking for/and then goes with you everywhere/like a shadow or a friend."

To acknowledge our own suffering and hold it with care and concern is to awaken self-compassion. Dr. Kristen Neff, pioneering educational researcher, teacher, and author of the book *Self-Compassion*, delineates three elements of self-compassion: self-kindness, common humanity, and mindfulness. Self-kindness replaces harsh self-judgment with understanding and care. Common humanity means recognizing that being imperfect and failing are part of being human and not our solitary burdens to bear. Mindfulness allows us to maintain a balanced perspective rather than overidentifying with our negative emotions. Together these three elements weave a resilient frame of mind, which allows us to deal with both difficult external circumstances and our own personal inadequacies and failures.

Neff explains that by simply placing our hand on our chest, we're able to tap into the mammalian caregiving system by triggering the release of oxytocin. This feel-good hormone increases feelings of trust and connectedness to self and others, calms stress and anxiety, and lowers the harmful effects of elevated cortisol levels.

STUDENT LESSON OBJECTIVES

- ✔ Notice what emotions feel like in the body.
- ✔ Give yourself a "self-compassion break."
- ✔ Do a close reading of the poem "Kindness" by Naomi Shihab Nye and answer questions about it.
- ✔ Write your own version of the poem or a story inspired by it.
- ✔ Write a paragraph sharing what you think the poet's message is and how it relates to your life.

Step 1: Quick Write (5 min.) and Partner Share (5 min.)

Prompt: Write about a time when you lost someone or something dear to you.

Step 2: Guided Mindfulness Practice (5–7 min.)

Teacher Note: This practice invites students to intentionally call to mind a loss they've experienced and offer themselves self-compassion. Before beginning, you may like to share a loss you've endured, the emotions it brought up for you, and how you met those emotions. Acknowledging what is challenging in your own life and your attempts to be a kind and gentle witness to your experience gives students the courage to also make friends with what is difficult in their own lives.

Script

Now take a few moments to let go of everything that has happened so far today. Allow yourself to be right here, right now, with no place to go, nothing to do, no one to be. Release any tension in your body—maybe in your toes, your belly, neck, and shoulders . . . roll your shoulders back and down, move your head from side to side. (Pause.) *Let go of any tension in your jaw, your forehead, behind your eyes.* (Pause.)

Listen to the bell. (Ring bell.) *Settle your body, your feet rooted in the earth, your back supported by your chair.* (Pause.) *Take a few deep breaths, and as much as possible, let go of any remaining tension in your body. Settle into this moment, this breath.*

Now, in your mind's eye, recall something or someone you've lost. It might be a soccer ball or an earring, or perhaps it is a more significant loss—a friendship, a relationship, a beloved pet or some other member of your family. Choose a loss that's around a five on a scale of one to ten—not the rawest experience, but something that feels workable to recall at this time. Notice any sensations that arise in your body, maybe a heaviness around your heart or a constriction in your throat. Allow whatever arises to just be there; witness it without trying to change it or push it away. In time, it will change.

If you feel comfortable doing so, place your hand on your heart in a gesture of kindness. (Pause.) *Recognize that you're not alone in feeling this way. Everyone experiences grief and loss. And offer yourself some kind words in silence, like you would share with a friend who was going through a hard time—"I'm here for you," or "It's okay to feel sad"—whatever words feel right to you.* (Pause and then invite a student to ring the bell.)

Step 3: Debrief (partners, then whole class, 5–10 min.)

Teacher Note: As mentioned in Lesson 2, it's important to let go of expectations regarding the discussion following the practice. Students may choose not to share about their loss, or they may be able to articulate much about their experiment with self-compassion. If you find yourself sharing a few more moments of silence with them, this is totally fine. Feel free to move on to Step 4. Students will be most receptive to hearing the words of the poem in this relaxed, open environment.

1. Were you able to recall a loss?
2. What sensations in your body were you aware of as you brought it to mind?
3. Could you offer yourself some kind words of support? What did you say to yourself?

Step 4: Read "Kindness" (2 min.)

Read poem aloud. Encourage students to visualize what they hear.

Step 5: Making Connections (5–10 min.)

1. What do you like about this poem?
2. What words or phrases do you remember?
3. What images stand out in your mind?

Step 6: Cloze Listening Activity (Handout A) (10 min.)

Discuss new vocabulary words. Then read the poem aloud a second time or have a student volunteer to do so, pausing while students fill in the missing words.

Step 7: Text-Dependent Questions (Handout B; Answers on Handout C) (15–20 min.)

Distribute Handout B for students to complete questions, either alone, with a partner, or in small groups.

Step 8: Text Response (Handout B; Sample Response on Handout C)

Prompt: For Nye, learning to be kind comes at a price. What message does she have for us about the suffering in our lives? What phrases does she use to convince us of its benefit?

Step 9: Self-Reflection

Prompt: In your own life, what experiences have taught you to be kind?

Step 10: Poem Writing (Handout D, E, or F) (10–15 min.)

Distribute Handout D, E, or F, depending on students' fluency in English and creative writing experience.

Step 11: Prose Writing Option

Prompt: Write a personal narrative reflecting on a significant loss and its meaning.

TAKEAWAY

Bringing students' lived experiences into the classroom requires courage—the courage to be able to maintain an open heart in the midst of suffering. Attending to our own losses with care prepares us to show up for them.

EXTENSION

The Day of the Dead is a Mexican tradition that occurs on November 1–2 (All Souls' Day, in some Christian traditions), in which families create altars in their homes to honor the memory of their deceased loved ones. Invite students to bring pictures of loved ones who have died as well as small treats to share. Creating intricate paper cutouts of flowers and skulls to make Mexican streamers is a mindful activity that many enjoy.

Kindness
by Naomi Shihab Nye

Before you know what kindness really is
you must lose things,
feel the future dissolve in a moment
like salt in a weakened broth.
5 What you held in your hand,
what you counted and carefully saved,
all this must go so you know
how desolate the landscape can be
between the regions of kindness.
10 How you ride and ride
thinking the bus will never stop,
the passengers eating maize and chicken
will stare out the window forever.

Before you learn the tender gravity of kindness
15 you must travel where the Indian in a white poncho
lies dead by the side of the road.
You must see how this could be you,
how he too was someone
who travelled through the night with plans
20 and the simple breath that kept him alive.

Before you know kindness as the deepest thing inside,
you must know sorrow as the other deepest thing.
You must wake up with sorrow.
You must speak to it till your voice
25 catches the thread of all sorrows
and you see the size of the cloth.
Then it is only kindness that makes sense anymore,
only kindness that ties your shoes
and sends you out into the day to buy bread,
30 only kindness that raises its head
from the crowd of the world to say
It is I you have been looking for,
and then goes with you everywhere
like a shadow or a friend.

Handout A

Cloze Listening Activity

Name: ______________________________

Listen to the poem and use the words to fill in the blanks.

shadow	salt	thinking	lies	sorrow
gravity	dissolve	desolate	journeyed	sense
lose	held	stare	kept	catches

Kindness

by Naomi Shihab Nye

Before you know what kindness really is
you must (1) __________________ things,
feel the future (2) __________________ in a moment
like (3) __________________ in a weakened broth.
5 What you (4) ______________________ in your hand,
what you counted and carefully saved,
all this must go so you know
how (5) ____________________ the landscape can be
between the regions of kindness.
10 How you ride and ride
(6) ______________________ the bus will never stop,
the passengers eating maize and chicken
will (7) ___________________ out the window forever.

Before you learn the tender (8) __________________ of kindness
15 you must travel where the Indian in a white poncho
(9) ________________ dead by the side of the road.
You must see how this could be you,
how he too was someone
who (10) __________________ through the night with plans
20 and the simple breath that (11) _________________ him alive.

Continued on next page

HANDOUT A 2 / 2

Before you know kindness as the deepest thing inside,
you must know (12) ___________________ as the other deepest thing.
You must wake up with sorrow.
You must speak to it till your voice
25 (13) _____________________ the thread of all sorrows
and you see the size of the cloth.
Then it is only kindness that makes (14) ________________ anymore,
only kindness that ties your shoes
and sends you out into the day to buy bread,
30 only kindness that raises its head
from the crowd of the world to say
It is I you have been looking for,
and then goes with you everywhere
like a (15) _____________________ or a friend.

Handout B

Text-Dependent Questions, Text Response, and Personal Reflection

Name: ______________________________

Text-Dependent Questions

1. A simile compares two unlike things using *like* or *as*. What does the poet compare loss to in line 4?

____

____

2. In lines 7–8, the speaker says, ". . . all this must go so you know how desolate the landscape can be between the regions of kindness." What does "desolate" mean? Use context clues. What mood is evoked by this image?

____

____

3. What did the poet see that taught her to be kind?

____

____

4. In the third stanza, the poet says: "you must know sorrow . . . you must speak to it till your voice/catches the thread of all sorrows/and you see the size of the cloth . . ." (22–26). What can we guess (infer) from these lines?

____

____

____

5. Repetition is an important element in the poem, used to create rhythm and structure. What phrase is repeated at the beginning of each stanza?

____

____

6. *Personification* is a figure of speech giving human attributes to an idea or an animal. What does kindness do for the speaker at the end of the poem? Cite textual evidence.

____

____

Continued on next page

Text Response

Examine the theme and its development in the poem. Cite textual evidence.

Prompt

For Nye, learning to be kind comes at a price. What message does she have for us about the suffering in our lives? What phrases does she use to convince us of its benefit?

____

____

____

____

____

Self-Reflection

In your own life, what experiences have taught you to be kind?

____

____

____

____

____

Handout C

Text-Dependent Questions Answer Key and Sample Text Response

Text-Dependent Questions Answer Key

1. "like salt in a weakened broth"
2. deserted; lonely, hopeless
3. She saw a dead man by the side of the road; she touched her own sadness.
4. By becoming intimate with her own sadness, she was able to become a more compassionate human being and recognize that she was not alone in her suffering, that sadness is part of the human condition.
5. "Before you know"; "Before you learn"; "Before you know"
6. Kindness acts as a compassionate caregiver/support. "Only kindness that ties your shoes/ and sends you out into the day to buy bread . . ."; "only kindness that raises its head/ from the crowd of the world to say . . ."

Sample Text Response

In the poem "Kindness," Nye illustrates the power of a life grounded in kindness and compassion. Acknowledging and accepting our own sorrow gives us strength. If we're able to dig beneath the habitual tendency to push away what is challenging or difficult and reflect on lessons learned, we become wiser. At the end of the poem, kindness "goes with you everywhere/like a shadow or a friend." This is living a life steeped in self-compassion and empathy.

Handout D

Basic Prose Writing Play Sheet

Name: ______________________________

Copy your favorite lines from the poem below:

____

____

Draw a picture of a sad moment in your life. Then, write a caption beneath it. Tell your story of losing something or someone important to you. Remember to answer the 5 Ws: Who? What? When? Where? and Why? (and How?)

I lost ____

This happened ____

I felt ____

Handout E

Intermediate Poem Writing Play Sheet

Name: ______________________________

Brainstorm words in the following categories, and then use your ideas to write your own version of the poem.

Things That Dissolve (e.g., rainbows, cough drops, dew)	Challenges in Your Life	Physical Gestures of Support	Words of Support

Continued on next page

HANDOUT E 2 / 2

Title: ____

(save the title for last and make it surprising or just right for your words)

Before you know what kindness really is

you must lose things,

feel the future dissolve in a moment

like ____,

(something that dissolves)

. . .

Before you know kindness as the deepest thing inside

you must know ____

(a challenge in your life)

Then it is only kindness that makes sense anymore,

only kindness that ____

(physical gesture of support)

only kindness that says ____

(words of support)

and then ____

(gesture of support)

Handout F

Advanced Poem Writing Play Sheet

Name: ______________________________

Use the following template as a guide to write your own version of the poem. Feel free to change it or abandon it at any point.

Title: ____

(save the title for last and make it surprising or just right for your words)

Before you know what kindness really is

you must lose things,

feel the future dissolve in a moment

like ____,

. . .

Before you know kindness as the deepest thing inside

you must know ____

Then it is only kindness that makes sense anymore.

only kindness that ____

only kindness that says ____

and then ____

CREATIVE WRITING EXAMPLES

Poetry

Heart Shield

Before you know what kindness really is
you must lose things,
feel the future dissolve in a moment
like clouds covering the sun,
. . .
Before you know kindness as the deepest thing inside
you must know that the inner thoughts cut deeper.
Then it is only kindness that makes sense anymore,
only kindness that hugs you when no one else is around
only kindness that says you're doing great, keep going!
and then attaches to your heart as a shield from everyone.

—Sammi, eleventh grade

What Kindness Is

Before you know what kindness really is, you must lose things.
Feel the future dissolving in a moment like sugar in strong coffee.
If you lose a family member like me, you will know.
One day the persons who you love and have in your hands
will never come back. That is very sad
and you start knowing what kindness is.

—Maria S., seventh grade, English learner

Feel the Air

Before you know what kindness really is, you must lose things.
Feel the fresh air on your face.
To learn to be mindful, you should take deep breaths.
You must breathe in.
You must breathe out.

Before you know kindness as the deepest thing inside
you must know the air is with you.
You must go outside and feel the breeze.

Then it is only kindness that matters.
You respect everything.

—Pedro H., seventh grade, English learner

Prose

Tenth Street Tragedy

I think it was Thanksgiving. My cousin and his friend Arturo were walking to the corner store to buy sodas and soups. All of a sudden someone started shooting at them. My cousin got shot on the leg and he couldn't walk, but they kept shooting. He was screaming and Arturo was running to help him. They shot Arturo three times and the last bullet hit his heart.

We heard the gunshots from my house, so my family and I went running to go see who got shot. When we got there, the car drove off. My aunt saw that it was her son lying on the sidewalk, and she hugged him and started to cry. We called the ambulance, and they came quick. My cousin was crying and saying, "This is my fault!" He got close to his friend and said, "I love you and I'll take care of you." Arturo said, "Take care. I love you too," and then he closed his eyes.

—Veronica T., seventh grade, English learner

REFERENCES, RESOURCES, AND FURTHER READING

Neff, Kristen D. "The Physiology of Self-Compassion." https://self-compassion.org/the-physiology-of-self-compassion/ (accessed August 1, 2022).

———. *Self-Compassion*. New York: William Morrow, 2011.

———. "The Three Components of Self-Compassion." Greater Good Science Center. Video of lecture, 6:18. Uploaded July 9, 2020. www.youtube.com/watch?v=11U0h0DPu7k (accessed August 1, 2022).

Neff, Kristin D., and Pittman McGehee. "Self-Compassion and Psychological Resilience among Adolescents and Young Adults." *Self and Identity* 9, no. 3 (June 2009): 225–40.

Nye, Naomi Shihab. "Kindness." Filmed at Wisdom Ways Center for Spirituality on March 18, 2016. Video of poetry reading, 4:44. www.youtube.com/watch?v=bBYzMsUVvtQ (accessed August 1, 2022).

Smith, Emily Esfahani. *The Power of Meaning: Crafting a Life That Matters*. New York: Crown, 2017. https://themoth.org/dispatches/storytelling-and-the-power-of-meaning (accessed August 1, 2022).

Lesson Six

Welcoming Difficult Emotions

"The Guest House" by Jalal al-Din Rumi

"Where your fear is, there is your task."

~ Carl Jung

OBJECTIVES

Mindfulness Skill	Identify challenging emotions and associated body sensations
CASEL Competencies Highlights	Self-awareness: identify one's emotions Self-management: manage one's emotions; identify and use self-management strategies
Creative Writing Task (Aligns with CCSS.ELA-LITERACY.W.9-10.3 a-e; W.9-10.4-6; L.9-10.1 a,b; L.9-10.2 a-c; L.9-10.3 a; ELD Part I, C, 10, 12 and ELD Part II, A-C)	Create a poem or personal narrative that explores challenging emotions
Academic Writing Task (Aligns with CCSS.ELA-LITERACY.W.9-10.1; W.9-10.4-6; L.9-10.1 a, b; L.9-10.2 a-c; L.9-10.3 a; ELD Part I, C, 11, 12 and ELD Part II, A-C)	Analyze theme and its development over course of poem

INTRODUCTION

"The Guest House" is a classic poem that addresses challenging emotions that knock us off our center. The reminder is that no emotion that enters our awareness is permanent. We need simply acknowledge what blips onto the screen without running from it, pushing it away, or sitting in judgment of ourselves for feeling it. By practicing patient acceptance of whatever arises, we free ourselves from the tyranny of our own minds.

DID YOU KNOW? WORKING WITH RESISTANCE

"The Guest House" encourages us to be gracious with challenging emotions rather than deny them or push them away. There's truth to the adage, "What we resist, persists." Mindfulness teacher and neuroscience research consultant Shinzen Young created the following mathematical equation to illustrate the power we have to lessen our suffering in the face of painful circumstances: *suffering = pain × resistance.*

While originally formulated to work with physical pain, this equation can be useful in discussing emotional pain, as well. None of us can escape feeling sad, anxious, angry, or any other human emotion. Where we do have agency is in how we relate to these challenging emotions. If we resist what's arising and want it to be different, this overlay of judgment that we add to our bare experience increases our misery. On the other hand, if we can allow the pain to be there, then we don't add the multiplying effect of resistance to the equation. Eventually we might even see it as an old friend or teacher.

STUDENT LESSON OBJECTIVES

- ✔ Explore how emotions show up in the body
- ✔ Offer yourself loving-kindness
- ✔ Do a close reading of the poem "The Guest House" by Rumi
- ✔ Write your own version of the poem or a story inspired by it
- ✔ Write a paragraph sharing what you think is the poet's message and find lines from the poem that show it

Step 1: Warm-Up and Quick Write

Warm-Up (2 min.)

Brainstorm a list of difficult emotions. Next ask students for a show of hands of who deals with anxiety, depression, anger, or feelings of inadequacy. *(This exercise allows young people to see that difficult emotions are part of being human and that no one escapes them.)*

Quick Write (5 min.) and Partner Share (5 min.)

Option 1

Prompt: Write about a strong emotion you sometimes feel. Where does it show up in your body? Is there any color, texture, sound, or image that goes along with it?

Option 2: Quick Draw

Prompt: Draw your "emotional house." Add favorite lines from the poem and emotions that sometimes challenge you. Then write three to five sentences describing your house.

Step 2: Guided Mindfulness Practice (5–7 min.)

Teacher Note: In this practice, students call to mind someone with whom they have had a difficult interaction recently, and the thoughts, feelings, and sensations that arise as they do so. As in the poem, the practice is to sit with difficult emotions, be friendly toward them, and allow them to dissipate on their own. If you're willing to share an example from your own life, that would be helpful.

Script

Now, take a moment to settle into your body, drop your ear to one shoulder without raising your shoulder to meet it, and then do this on the other side. Maybe take a twist in your chair and then feel your seat. (Ring bell.) *Ground yourself with your breath coming and going. As a community, let's take three deep inhalations and exhalations together. Breathing in . . . and breathing out. Breathing in . . . and breathing out. In . . . and out. Now breathe naturally, using your breath as an anchor, or whatever works best for you—maybe sounds or the felt sense of sitting in your chair.* (Pause.)

As you settle, become aware of what's going on with you on the inside, as if you were a meteorologist reporting the weather. Maybe it's sunny and bright or cloudy with a chance of rain. (Pause.) *Just simply notice what's going on within you right now, without judgment or the need to change anything.* (Pause.)

Now, when you're ready, call to mind someone with whom you've had difficulty during the past week, maybe a parent or a sibling or one of your classmates. If you've had a major fight with someone, you may want to choose a memory that's less intense. Maybe it was something you saw on social media. (Pause.) *When you've chosen one memory, notice what thoughts and feelings arise. See if you can sense where these feelings show up in your body.* (Pause.) *Perhaps you can detect a tightening in your belly or a sinking or heavy feeling in your chest.* (Pause.) *There's no right answer. Just notice with kind attention what happens in your body and mind as you recall the memory*. (Pause.)

As you stay with this memory, check in with your thoughts, feelings, and body sensations now. Oftentimes, if we give ourselves some quiet space to explore what's going on with us, our internal weather changes on its own. (Pause.) *Either way, whatever you're noticing, simply allow it to be there and hold it with kindness.*

Now let go of that memory and wish yourself well. You might like to repeat these simple phrases to yourself: "May I be happy. May I be at ease in my body and mind. May I be safe from inner and outer harm. May I be well." (Pause.) *"May I be happy. May I be at ease in my body and mind. May I be safe from inner and outer harm. May I be well."* (Pause.) *You can repeat these words or any that feel right for you.* (Pause.) *And if you feel able, also wish well to the person you brought to mind: "May they be happy. May they be at ease in their body and mind. May they be safe from inner and outer harm."* (Pause for a minute or so.) *Now ground yourself again with your body and breath.* (Invite a student to ring the bell.)

Step 3: Debrief (partners, then whole class, 5–10 min.)

1. Could you call to mind a difficult interaction with someone?
2. What emotion(s) came up for you when you recalled this interaction?
3. Where did you feel the emotion in your body?

Step 4: Read "The Guest House" (1 min.)

Read poem aloud. Encourage students to visualize what they hear.

Step 5: Connect with the Poem (5–10 min.)

1. What do you like about the poem? What feels lit up for you?
2. What words or phrases do you remember?
3. What images stand out in your mind?

Step 6: Cloze Listening Activity (10 min.)

Discuss new vocabulary words. Then read the poem aloud a second time or have a student volunteer do so, pausing while students fill in the missing words.

Step 7: Text-Dependent Questions (Handout B; Answers on Handout C) (15–20 min.)

Distribute Handout B for students to complete questions, either alone, with a partner, or in small groups.

Step 8: Text Response (Handout B; Sample Response on Handout C)

Prompt: Why did Rumi title his poem "The Guest House"? Write a paragraph in which you discuss the theme.

Step 9: Self-Reflection (Handout B)

Prompt: Write about a time when you faced a fear or challenged a negative thought you had.

Step 10: Poem Writing (Handout D, E, or F) (10–15 min.)

Distribute Handout D, E, or F, depending on students' fluency in English and creative writing experience.

Step 11: Prose Writing Option

Teacher Note: As student writing may include sensitive personal material, reassure them that they always have the option to decline sharing with the class.

Prompt: Write about a specific time you experienced the strong emotion you mentioned in your quick write. Where did you notice it in your body? What did you say and do? What was the outcome? Reflecting upon it now, is there anything you would have changed?

TAKEAWAY

"Name it to tame it" is a common expression used in mindfulness circles. Originally coined by neuropsychiatrist Daniel Siegel, this dictum refers to the power of labeling what's occurring in our bodies and minds when we're flooded by strong emotions. By putting our bare experience into words, we create a "story" of who we or others are, and we are better able to regulate our emotions. Then we can investigate what thoughts may be feeding the flames of these challenging emotions and sense how the drama is playing out in our bodies.

EXTENSION

By looking clearly at our fear, sadness, anger, jealousy, and disappointment, we're also able to investigate what stressors in our current life situation may be causing these challenging emotions. This analysis may help us to accept what is present in the moment and allow the emotions to pass through. Sonia Lupien at the Center for Studies on Human Stress created the insightful acronym NUTS to help identify causes of stress:

- Novelty
- Unpredictability
- Threat to the ego
- Sense of control

Give students the opportunity to put pen to paper, to "spill the tea" of what they're feeling, and allow them the space to investigate what changes, unknowns, or threats may be causing them to feel unstable. This journaling activity can give them a greater perspective on their current situation. They can then conclude that their predicament is temporary and will change. As the poem so beautifully illustrates, emotions come and go.

The Guest House
by Rumi

This being human is a guest house.
Every morning a new arrival.

A joy, a depression, a meanness,
some momentary awareness comes
5 As an unexpected visitor.
Welcome and entertain them all!
Even if they're a crowd of sorrows,
who violently sweep your house
empty of its furniture,
10 still treat each guest honorably.
He may be clearing you out
for some new delight.

The dark thought, the shame, the malice,
meet them at the door laughing,
15 and invite them in.

Be grateful for whoever comes,
because each has been sent
as a guide from beyond.

HANDOUT A

Handout A

Cloze Listening Activity

Name: ______________________________

Listen to the poem and use the words to fill in the blanks.

sweep	malice	they're	delight	entertain	grateful
arrival	guide	awareness	depression	invite	treat

The Guest House
by Rumi

This being human is a guest house.
Every morning a new (1) ______________________.

A joy, a (2) ______________________, a meanness,
some momentary (3) ______________________ comes
5 As an unexpected visitor.

Welcome and (4) ______________________ them all!
Even if (5) ______________________ a crowd of sorrows,
who violently (6) ______________________ your house
empty of its furniture,
10 still (7) ______________________ each guest honorably.
He may be clearing you out
for some new (8) ______________________.

The dark thought, the shame, the (9) ______________________,
meet them at the door laughing,
15 and (10) ______________________ them in.

Be (11) ______________________ for whoever comes,
because each has been sent
as a (12) ______________________ from beyond.

Handout B

Text-Dependent Questions, Text Response, and Personal Reflection

Name: ______________________________

Text-Dependent Questions

1. List six emotions mentioned in the poem.

____

____

2. In Spanish, *mal* means bad. Does the word "malice" have a positive or negative feeling (connotation)? Define it.

____

____

3. The poet speaks of emotions as guests. Find two other words (nouns) he uses to describe them in a positive way.

____

____

4. In the third stanza, the speaker says, "Even if they're a crowd of sorrows,/who violently sweep your house /empty of its furniture,/still treat each guest honorably./He may be clearing you out/for some new delight" (7–12). What can we guess (infer) the poet is saying about what difficult emotions can offer us?

____

____

____

5. What is a guest house? Why is it an appropriate comparison (metaphor) for us as human beings?

____

____

____

6. Personification means giving human qualities to something that is not human or to an abstract quality. What does "the crowd of sorrows" do in line 8?

____

____

Continued on next page

Text Response

Examine the theme and its development in the poem. Cite textual evidence.

Prompt

Why did Rumi title his poem “The Guest House”? Write a paragraph in which you discuss the theme. Be sure to include lines from the poem (textual evidence).

Self-Reflection

Write about a time when you faced a fear or challenged a negative thought you had.

Handout C

Text-Dependent Questions Answer Key and Sample Text Response

Text-Dependent Questions Answer Key

1. Joy, depression, meanness, sorrow, shame, malice, gratitude
2. Negative; wishing to hurt someone
3. Visitor, guide
4. *Answers will vary.* There may be a silver lining—something good that can come from difficult experiences, if we stay open, curious, and willing to learn and grow; when we experience a loss, if we can learn to let go, something better may take its place.
5. A place where travelers stay; our emotions come and go
6. “sweeps your house empty of its furniture”

Sample Text Response

Rumi titled his poem “The Guest House” because he is encouraging us to be kind and welcoming toward all the emotions we feel. Toward the end of the poem, he says, “The dark thought, the shame, the malice,/meet them at the door laughing,/and invite them in.” By meeting challenging emotions bravely, rather than pushing them away, attempting to distract ourselves from feeling them, or going numb, we become masters of our emotions rather than their slaves.

Handout D

Basic Poem Writing Play Sheet

Name: ______________________________

Copy your favorite line from "The Guest House" below:

____

Now brainstorm three to five words in each category:

Meeting Places	People Who Meet There	Emotions	Positive Qualities

Next, use your ideas to write your own version of the poem.

Title: ____
(save the title for last and make it surprising or just right for your words)

This being human is a ____________________________________.
(place where people gather)

Every morning a new ____________________________________.
(person who goes there)

__________________, __________________, __________________
(emotion 1) *(emotion 2)* *(emotion 3)*

Welcome and entertain them all!

They may be there to teach you ____________________________________.
(positive quality)

Continued on next page

Draw a picture to accompany your poem.

Handout E

Intermediate Poem Writing Play Sheet

Name: ______________________________

Brainstorm words in the following categories, and then use your ideas to write your own version of the poem.

Meeting Places	People Who Meet There	Forces of Nature	Synonyms for "Destroy"	Kind Acts

Continued on next page

Title: ____

(save the title for last and make it surprising or just right for your words)

This being human is a ______________________________________.

(meeting place)

Every morning a new ______________________________________.

(someone who arrives there)

____________________, ____________________, ____________________ come.

(emotion 1) *(emotion 2)* *(emotion 3)*

Welcome and entertain them all!

Even if they're a ____________________ of ____________________

(something powerful) *(emotion)*

who ____,

(personify the emotion: What destructive thing does it do?)

still ____.

(kind action)

S/he may be ____

(What positive thing could this emotion be doing?)

Be grateful for whoever comes,

because ____.

(Why should we welcome challenging emotions?)

Handout F

Advanced Poem Writing Play Sheet

Name: ______________________________

Use the following template as a guide to write your own version of the poem. Feel free to change it or abandon it at any point.

Title: ____

(save the title for last and make it surprising or just right for your words)

This being human is a ____.

Every morning a new ____.

______________________, ______________________, ______________________ come.

Welcome and entertain them all!

Even if they're a ______________________ of ______________________

who ____,

still ____.

S/he may be ____

Be grateful for whoever comes,

because ____.

CREATIVE WRITING EXAMPLES

Poetry

This being human is a city.
Every morning traffic jams, donuts, the homeless
fear, worry, depression, happiness, delight.

Welcome and entertain them all!
Even if they're drug dealers
who have guns and smoke weed,
still offer them holy water.

Be grateful to whoever comes
because they are still part of the city.

—Collaborative poem, seventh grade, English learners

This being human is a BART station.
Every morning a new passenger
joy, anger, disgust come.

Welcome and entertain them all!
Even if she's a flood of loneliness
who drowns your car,
still give her a pat on the back.
She may be there to teach you compassion.

Be grateful for whoever comes
because she will go away soon.

—Collaborative poem, seventh grade, English learners

Prose

The Last Day with Cinnamon

It was not long ago that my dog went missing. She was a chihuahua named Cinnamon. Her fur was medium length and the color of an orange, but not an ordinary orange, a majestic orange. Cinnamon was the kindest dog you could ever meet, and she was light on her feet.

One day she went missing. I saw a neon-yellow, thin paper on my door. My eyes were horrified and blurred, the tears running like two rivers down my face. The paper said she was in the pound and described her in great detail, so much so it was as if I could see her in my head.

My mom and I went as fast as possible to the pound to get her, but we found out it was going to cost hundreds of dollars. My mom said to let it go, but I couldn't. It was a nightmare I never woke up from. Even today I'm still in that terrifying nightmare even if I appear to be calm.

—Anthony, seventh grade, English learner

REFERENCES, RESOURCES, AND FURTHER READING

Carter, Christine. "Dear Christine: How Can I Help My Stressed-Out Teenager?" https://greatergood.berkeley.edu/article/item/dear_christine_how_can_i_help_my_stressed_out_teenager (accessed September 26, 2021).

Heart-Mind Online. "N.U.T.S.: Understanding Stress." https://heartmindonline.org/resources/nuts-understanding-stress (accessed October 29, 2021).

Lindsay, E. K., B. Chin, C. M. Greco, S. Young, K. W. Brown, A. G. C. Wright, J. M. Smyth, D. Burkett, and J. D. Creswell. "How Mindfulness Training Promotes Positive Emotions: Dismantling Acceptance Skills Training in Two Randomized Controlled Trials." *J Pers Soc Psycholo*gy 115, no. 6 (December 2018): 944–73.

Lupien, S. J., I. Ouellet-Morin, L. Trépanier, R. P. Juster, M. F. Marin, N. Francois, S. Sindi, N. Wan, H. Findlay, N. Durand, L. Cooper, T. Schramek, J. Andrews, V. Corbo, K. Dedovic, B. Lai, and P. Plusquellec. "*The DeStress for Success Program*: Effects of a Stress Education Program on Cortisol Levels and Depressive Symptomatology in Adolescents Making the Transition to High School." *Neuroscience* 249 (September 2013): 74–87.

Rumi, Jalal al-Din. "The Guest House." Calm. Video montage and poetry reading, 0:59. Uploaded March 29, 2019. www.youtube.com/watch?v=_SMcuZfUqG0 (accessed August 1, 2022).

Siegel, Daniel J. *The Whole-Brain Child.* New York: Bantam, 2012.

Young, Shinzen. "Meditation: Escaping into Life." Interview with Michael Toms. Last modified December 7, 2019. www.shinzen.org/wp-content/uploads/2016/12/art_escape.pdf.

———. "On Compassion, Equanimity and Impermanence." Last modified January 25, 2019. www.dailygood.org/story/2213/on-compassion-equanimity-and-impermanence-shinzen-young.

———. *The Science of Enlightenment*. Boulder, CO: Sounds True, 2016.

Lesson Seven

Acceptance

"So Much Happiness" by Naomi Shihab Nye

"Happiness is the absence of striving for happiness."

~ Chuang Tzu

OBJECTIVES

Mindfulness Skills	Cultivate an open, receptive attitude toward whatever is present Practice gratitude
CASEL Competencies Highlight	Social awareness: Recognize and express gratitude for family, friends, and other positive relationships
Creative Writing Task (Aligns with CCSS.ELA-LITERACY.W.9-10.3 a-e; W.9-10.4-6; L.9-10.1 a,b; L.9-10.2 a-c; L.9-10.3 a; ELD Part I, C, 10, 12 and ELD Part II, A-C)	Compose a poem or story reflecting upon both the joys and challenges in one's life
Academic Writing Task (Aligns with CCSS.ELA-LITERACY.W.9-10.1; W.9-10.4-6; L.9-10.1 a, b; L.9-10.2 a-c; L.9-10.3 a; ELD Part I, C, 11, 12 and ELD Part II, A-C)	Analyze theme and its development in the poem

INTRODUCTION

Being mindful means being aware of what's happening, before we apply our likes and dislikes, before we color reality with our judgments. We accept, for the moment, that this is how things are. From this place of stillness and nonreactivity, clarity arises, and we are better able to see what the next good step is. The poem "So Much Happiness" points to this understanding when the speaker says that happiness "doesn't need anything." If we can learn to accept whatever is present in the moment and know that it will change, we can truly cultivate a happy heart.

DID YOU KNOW? SELF-DIRECTED NEUROPLASTICITY

Our minds are like Teflon for positive experiences and like Velcro for negative ones. Neuropsychologist Rick Hanson uses these analogies to describe our innate negativity bias: The brain is predisposed to look for and react to negative information, and then it stores and retrieves it more readily than positive information. Why? To help us survive. Our negativity bias has kept us on alert for tigers hiding in bushes. It's also part of our two-million-year-old tribal propensity to see those who are different from us as potential threats. Unlike positive experiences, which quickly fade from our memory, negative experiences are intensely focused on and stored in our bank of "implicit memory," which constitutes our feeling of being alive. As the stockpile of negative experiences grows, this feeling of being alive grows dimmer and dimmer.

The good news is we can change our brains. This is called self-directed neuroplasticity. To override our negativity bias, Hanson recommends "soaking in the good." With awareness and intention, we can hang on to positive experiences, savor them, feel them in our bodies and our emotions, and then sense and intend that they are being absorbed by our brains and bodies and registering deeply in our emotional memory. Visualizing these positive vibes as precious jewels, which we place in our hearts, or as a golden light that bathes us, can help us to integrate them into our mind-body experience.

STUDENT LESSON OBJECTIVES

- ✔ Practice taking in the good by calling to mind someone for whom you're grateful
- ✔ Do a close reading of the poem "So Much Happiness" by Naomi Shihab Nye and answer questions about it
- ✔ Write your own version of the poem or a story inspired by it
- ✔ Write a paragraph sharing what you think the poet's message is and how it relates to your life

Step 1: Quick Write (5 min.) and Partner Share (5 min.)

Prompt: Write a list of ten things for which you're grateful.

Step 2: Guided Mindfulness Practice (5–7 min.)

Teacher Note: As always, begin the practice by inviting students to tune into their bodies and their breath. Next, invite them to call to mind someone and something for which they are grateful and bathe in the positive feelings that arise.

Script

Take a moment to settle into your body. Maybe move your head from side to side, relaxing and releasing any tension in the neck and shoulders. Open and close the jaw, releasing any tightness there. And soften the muscles of the forehead and around the eyes. Allow the weight of gravity to anchor you to your seat and support you.

Listen to the bell. (Ring bell.) *Take an upright, relaxed posture with your feet rooted in the floor. Allow your eyes to gently close or soften your gaze. Now take a few slow, deep breaths. Notice your belly and chest rise as you inhale, then fall as you exhale.* (Pause.) *And for a few minutes, allow whatever arises in your heart and mind—worries or plans, memories or regrets—just to be there without clinging to them or pushing them away. Just acknowledge and allow, acknowledge and allow, knowing that whatever arises will eventually pass away.*

Now call to mind something for which you're grateful—waking up this morning, the breath in your body, all your organs sustaining you . . . the warm, comfortable bed in which you slept, maybe something you ate or drank for breakfast, or a snack a friend shared with you at the break. (Pause.)

Now call to mind someone for whom you feel grateful—it may be a parent or grandparent, a friend, or a pet. You might whisper their name to yourself or use a short description to help you keep focused. (Pause.) *Think of someone who makes you smile or laugh, who gives you a hug or holds your hand. Imagine looking into their tender, loving face, their soft eyes. Breathe in the positive feelings you notice, maybe calm, ease, joy. . . . Feel it in your heart center as you bathe in their love for you.* (Pause.) *Maybe the edges of your mouth curl upward as you imagine them looking into your eyes. Now take a moment to express gratitude for this person or pet, and for anything else you wish to at this time.* (Invite a student to ring the bell.)

Step 3: Debrief (partners, then whole class, 5–10 min.)

Teacher Note: Just a reminder to take a gentle approach here. Students may or may not wish to share. They could be given the option of writing about their experience and reading to a partner first. Or feel free to move on to Step 4.

1. How do you feel after practicing gratitude?
2. Whom or what did you call to mind?
3. How did it feel to imagine receiving their love? What did you notice in your body?

Step 4: Read "So Much Happiness" (2 min.)

Read poem aloud. Encourage students to visualize what they hear.

Step 5: Making Connections (5–10 min.)

1. What do you appreciate about this poem?
2. What words or phrases do you remember?
3. How do you feel after hearing it?

Step 6: Cloze Listening Activity Worksheet (10 min.)

Discuss new vocabulary words. Then read the poem aloud a second time or have a student volunteer do so, pausing while students fill in the missing words.

Step 7: Text-Dependent Questions (Handout B; Answers on Handout C) (15–20 min.)

Distribute Handout B for students to complete questions, either alone, with a partner, or in small groups.

Step 8: Text Response (Handout B; Sample Response on Handout C)

Prompt: How does Nye suggest we may find true happiness? What phrases does she use to convince us?

Step 9: Self-Reflection

Prompt: Can you be happy even when things don't go as you would like? How? Give an example from your life.

Step 10: Poem Writing

Brainstorm (10–15 min.)

Ask each small group to create a list for one of the following categories: good memories, present concerns, favorite foods, chores or other burdens, and ways they practice self-care. Have a spokesperson share their list with the whole class.

Poem Writing (Handout D, E, or F) (10–15 min.)

Distribute Handout D, E, or F, depending on students' fluency in English and creative writing experience.

Step 11: Prose Writing Option

Prompt: Write about someone in your life for whom you're grateful.

TAKEAWAY

This lesson gives students a safe way to share what is difficult or challenging in their lives, and it encourages them to adopt a healthy, positive outlook in spite of it all. Rather than seeing themselves as victims of their circumstances, they can choose happiness. This practice of developing acceptance and gratitude will serve them for a lifetime.

EXTENSION

Watch the music video "Happy" by Pharrell Williams. Invite students to stand while they watch and join in if they like. Then have them write about something that makes them feel like "a room without a roof."

So Much Happiness
by Naomi Shihab Nye

It is difficult to know what to do with so much happiness.
With sadness there is something to rub against,
a wound to tend with lotion and cloth.
When the world falls in around you, you have pieces to pick up,
5 something to hold in your hands, like ticket stubs or change.
But happiness floats.
It doesn't need you to hold it down.
It doesn't need anything.
Happiness lands on the roof of the next house, singing,
10 and disappears when it wants to.
You are happy either way.
Even the fact that you once lived in a peaceful tree house
and now live over a quarry of noise and dust
cannot make you unhappy.
15 Everything has a life of its own,
it too could wake up filled with possibilities
of coffee cake and ripe peaches,
and love even the floor which needs to be swept,
the soiled linens and scratched records . . .
20 Since there is no place large enough
to contain so much happiness,
you shrug, you raise your hands, and it flows out of you
into everything you touch. You are not responsible.
You take no credit, as the night sky takes no credit
25 for the moon, but continues to hold it, and share it,
and in that way, be known.

Handout A

Cloze Listening Activity

Name: ______________________________

Listen to the poem and use the words to fill in the blanks.

change	contain	difficult	disappears	either	floats	flows
hold	known	lands	peaceful	peaches	pick	possibilities
sadness	shrug	soiled	swept	quarry	wound	

So Much Happiness
by Naomi Shihab Nye

It is (1) __________________ to know what to do with so much happiness.
With (2) __________________ there is something to rub against,
a (3) __________________ to tend with lotion and cloth.
When the world falls in around you, you have pieces to (4) __________________ up
5 something to hold in your hands, like ticket stubs or (5) __________________.
But happiness (6) __________________.
It doesn't need you to (7) __________________ it down.
It doesn't need anything.
Happiness (8) __________________ on the roof of the next house, singing,
10 and (9) __________________ when it wants to.
You are happy (10) __________________ way.
Even the fact that you once lived in a (11) __________________ tree house
and now live over a (12) __________________ of noise and dust
cannot make you unhappy.
15 Everything has a life of its own,
it too could wake up filled with (13) __________________
of coffee cake and ripe (14) __________________
and love even the floor which needs to be (15) __________________,
the (16) __________________ linens and scratched records . . .

Continued on next page

20 Since there is no place large enough
to (17) ________________ so much happiness,
you (18) _____________, you raise your hands, and it (19) _____________ out of you
into everything you touch. You are not responsible.
You take no credit, as the night sky takes no credit
25 for the moon, but continues to hold it, and share it,
and in that way, be (20) ________________.

Handout B

Text-Dependent Questions, Text Response, and Personal Reflection

Name: ______________________________

Text-Dependent Questions

1. What's surprising (ironic) about the first line of the poem: "It is difficult to know what to do with so much happiness"?

____

____

2. What is sadness compared to in line 3 (a metaphor)? What does this imagery suggest we must do with our sadness?

____

____

3. In line 13, the poet says, "Even the fact that you once lived in a peaceful tree house/and now live over a quarry of noise and dust/cannot make you unhappy." As it's used here, does the word "quarry" have a positive or negative feeling (connotation)? What does "quarry" mean? Use context clues.

____

____

4. Consider the line: "Happiness lands on the roof of the next house, singing, and disappears when it wants to" (9–10). What concrete thing do you imagine happiness to be?

____

____

5. The poet mentions waking up to "coffee cake." Name two other things mentioned in the poem that make the speaker happy.

____

____

6. The root word of equanimity is *equa*, meaning "the same." Cite evidence from the poem that shows that the poet is equanimous, or calm and composed under all circumstances.

____

____

Continued on next page

Text Response

Examine the theme of the poem and its development.

Prompt

How does Nye suggest we may find true happiness? What phrases does she use to convince us? (Cite textual evidence.)

____

____

____

____

____

____

Self-Reflection

Can you be happy even when things don't go as you would like? How? Give an example from your life.

____

____

____

____

____

____

Handout C

Text-Dependent Questions Answer Key and Sample Text Response

Text-Dependent Questions Answer Key

1. *Answers will vary.* Normally, being happy is not a problem; people may have difficulty trusting feeling happy because of hardships in the past; when people have too much happiness, they may take it for granted.
2. A wound; be gentle and caring with it
3. Negative; a mining pit
4. *Answers will vary.* A bird, a fluffy cloud, a cloud of smoke, Santa
5. ripe peaches, the floor which needs to be swept, soiled linens, scratched records
6. According to the *Merriam-Webster Dictionary*, *equanimity* means "evenness of mind, especially under stress"; "Happiness lands on the roof of the next house, singing, and disappears when it wants to./You are happy either way"; "once lived in a peaceful tree house/ and now live over a quarry of noise and dust"; "love even the floor which needs to be swept,/ the soiled linens and scratched records"

Sample Text Response

Nye suggests that it's possible to see all situations in a positive light. In lines 9–11 she writes, "Happiness lands on the roof of the next house, singing, and disappears when it wants to./You are happy either way." This demonstrates the quality of equanimity, a calm composure that one can develop as a healthy habit of mind. Even stressful situations, such as finding yourself living "over a quarry of noise and dust," cannot shake it. This variety of happiness has great power to affect not only your own life, but also the lives of those around you. It has a beautiful, luminescent quality like the moon, which she alludes to in the final lines of the poem: "You take no credit, as the night sky takes no credit for the moon."

Handout D

Basic Poem Writing Play Sheet

Name: ______________________________

Brainstorm ideas in the columns below and then use them to write your own version of the poem.

Good Things That Happened to You in the Past	Challenges in Your Life Now

Continued on next page

Title: ____

(save the title for last and make it surprising or just right for your words)

It is difficult to know what to do with so much happiness.

Even the fact that you once ____

(something good that happened to you in the past)

and now ____

(something difficult in your life now)

cannot make you unhappy.

Draw pictures of important moments in your life: one from the past, and one from the present.

The Past	Now

Handout E

Intermediate Poem Writing Play Sheet

Name: ______________________________

Title: ____
(save the title for last and make it surprising or just right for your words)

It is difficult to know what to do with so much happiness.

Even the fact that you once ____
(something wonderful that happened to you)

and now ____
(something difficult in your life)

cannot make you unhappy.

Everything has a life of its own,

it too could wake up filled with possibilities

of _________________________________ and ______________________________
(yummy food) *(yummy food)*

and love even _________________________________,
(chore or burden)

___________________________________, and ___________________________________.
(chore or burden) *(chore or burden)*

Since there is no place large enough

to contain so much happiness, _____________________________________,
(action verb—what you do to stay positive)

_____________________________________, and _____________________________________.
(action verb—what you do to stay positive) *(action verb—what you do to stay positive)*

Handout F

Advanced Poem Writing Play Sheet

Name: ______________________________

Use the following template as a guide to write your own version of the poem. Feel free to change it or abandon it at any point.

Title: ____

(save the title for last and make it surprising or just right for your words)

It is difficult to know what to do with so much happiness.

Even the fact that you once ____

and now ____

cannot make you unhappy.

Everything has a life of its own,

it too could wake up filled with possibilities

of ______________________________ and ______________________________

and love even ____,

_________________________________, and ___________________________________.

Since there is no place large enough

to contain so much happiness, _________________________________,

_________________________________, and _________________________________.

CREATIVE WRITING EXAMPLES

Poetry

What Makes Happiness

It is difficult to know what to do with so much happiness.
Even the fact that you once got into art schools,
and now struggle to wake up,
cannot make you unhappy.

Everything has a life of its own,
it too could wake up filled with possibilities
of strawberries and cookies
and love even washing dishes, cleaning floors, and doing laundry.

Since there is no place large enough
to contain so much happiness,
draw, dance, and eat.

—Nazia, eleventh grade

It is difficult to know what to do with so much happiness.
Even the fact that you once heard your family laughing
and now hear them yelling at each other
cannot make you unhappy.

Everything has a life of its own,
it too could wake up filled with possibilities
of tamales and horchata
and love even scrubbing the floor, washing dishes, and cleaning your room.

Since there is no place large enough
to contain so much happiness,
help people in need, help your family,
and take care of yourself.

—Sophia G., seventh grade, English learner

Prose

The Best Mom, Maria

My mom is the best mom because she has fought hard to give us a good future. She works day and night to give us food, clothes, and shoes. Sometimes she sends money to my dad in Mexico to buy food for my sister and my nephews. . . . I am very proud of my mother because she never takes living in the U.S. for granted. No matter what happens, she doesn't stop fighting for a good future for my sister and me.

—Enrique, seventh grade, English learner

REFERENCES, RESOURCES, AND FURTHER READING

Hanson, Rick. *Hardwiring Happiness: The New Brain Science of Contentment, Calm, and Confidence.* New York: Harmony Books, 2013.

———. "How To Trick Your Brain For Happiness." https://greatergood.berkeley.edu/article/item/how_to_trick_your_brain_for_happiness (accessed September 26, 2021).

———. "Pet the Lizard." www.rickhanson.net/pet-the-lizard/?highlight=implicit%20memory%20negativity%20bias (accessed September 26, 2021).

———. "Positive Neuroplasticity." In *Advances in Contemplative Psychotherapy,* edited by Joseph Loizzo, Miles Neale, and Emily Wolf. New York: Routledge, 2017.

———. "Take in the Good." www.rickhanson.net/take-in-the-good/ (accessed September 26, 2021).

Nye, Naomi Shihab. "Naomi Shihab Nye on What Inspires Her Poetry." Academy of American Poets. Video of conversation, 3:18. Uploaded September 29, 2015. www.youtube.com/watch?v=5gDZefjvQ-0 (accessed August 1, 2022).

Williams, Pharrell. "Happy." Directed by Mimi Valdes. Music video. Uploaded November 21, 2013. www.youtube.com/watch?v=y6Sxv-sUYtM (accessed August 1, 2022).

Lesson Eight

Befriending Oneself

"Love After Love" by Derek Walcott

"What I am looking for is not out there, it is in me."

~ Helen Keller

OBJECTIVES

<table>
<tr><td>Mindfulness Skills</td><td>Investigate one's inner dialogue

Practice self-compassion</td></tr>
<tr><td>CASEL Framework Competencies Highlight</td><td>Self-awareness
• Identify personal assets
• Link feelings, values, and thoughts</td></tr>
<tr><td>Creative Writing Task

(Aligns with CCSS.ELA-LITERACY.W.9-10.3 a-e; W.9-10.4-6; L.9-10.1 a,b; L.9-10.2 a-c; L.9-10.3 a; ELD Part I, C, 10, 12 and ELD Part II, A-C)</td><td>Produce a piece of writing that celebrates the ways one nurtures oneself in body, mind, and spirit</td></tr>
<tr><td>Academic Writing Task

(Aligns with CCSS.ELA-LITERACY.W.9-10.1; W.9-10.4-6; L.9-10.1 a, b; L.9-10.2 a-c; L.9-10.3 a; ELD Part I, C, 11, 12 and ELD Part II, A-C)</td><td>Analyze theme and its development in poem</td></tr>
</table>

INTRODUCTION

How do we fall in love with ourselves again? In *The Four Agreements*, renowned spiritual teacher Don Miguel Ruiz revives the ancient, indigenous Toltec philosophy from southern Mexico, a code of conduct that can help us live a life grounded in self-love, self-compassion, and freedom. In the first agreement, "Be impeccable with your word," Ruiz emphasizes the power words have to create realities. The Latin origin of the word "impeccable" is pecatus, which means sin, so to be impeccable means to be without sin. According to the Toltec tradition, a sin is anything we feel or believe, say, or do that goes against ourselves. To be impeccable with our word means to cease from judging and blaming ourselves and to use our energy in the direction of truth and self-love. We do take responsibility for our actions, but we do not reject ourselves.

This sentiment is echoed in Derek Walcott's poem "Love After Love." When we lose ourselves and begin seeking love outside ourselves that only we can give, we would do well to remember who we really are. This is precisely what the speaker in the poem is asking us to do: "Take down the love letters from the bookshelf, the photographs, the desperate notes"—to remember where we came from, to remember that we *are* love.

DID YOU KNOW? HEART-HEALTHY SELF-TALK

There has been an explosion in research on self-compassion since Kristin Neff's first study published in 2003. And for good reason. Being kind to ourselves and less judgmental has been found to decrease mental health disorders and increase positive well-being in both adults and adolescents. One study found that the psychophysiological response of self-compassion included decreased nervous system arousal and increased parasympathetic activation. This means that practicing self-compassion results in a decrease in heart rate and an increase in heart rate variability (where the amount of time between heartbeats fluctuates slightly), patterns linked to effective emotion regulation in times of stress.

STUDENT LESSON OBJECTIVES

- ✔ Practice observing thoughts and emotions that arise during mindfulness practice, particularly self-judgments, and offer yourself self-compassion
- ✔ Do a close reading of the poem "Love After Love" by Derek Walcott and answer questions about it
- ✔ Write your own version of the poem or a story inspired by it
- ✔ Write a paragraph sharing what you think the poet's message is and refer to lines from the poem to show it

Step 1: Warm-Up (5 min.) and Quick Write (5 min.)

Warm-Up

Do a whip-around, having students share one thing they like about themselves.

Quick Write

Prompt: What's something you enjoy doing that nurtures you in body and mind?

Step 2: Guided Practice (5–7 min.)

Teacher Note: This practice traverses some rocky inner terrain—our own self-judgments and negative self-talk. Remind students to take care of themselves, leaving their eyes open if they like and choosing a safe, comfortable anchor of attention, whether it be body sensations, the breath, or sounds, colors, or shapes in their environment.

Script

Let's begin by appreciating your efforts to arrive here in this moment, aware of the challenges we have to deal with just to show up on some days, to bring body, mind, and heart together in this very place and time. . . . (Pause.) *It's not easy to remember to pause in the world in which we live. There's a lot of doing, lots of running around, completing our tasks. And practicing simply being goes against the stream, so honor yourself for your courage and determination to practice self-care. If you like, set an intention for your practice today: "May I stand with myself," or "May I be at ease," or whatever words feel right to you.*

Now bring your full attention to the sound of the bell from the very beginning to the very end, when the bell is still. (Ring bell three times.) *Now notice your body in this space, where your back and hips contact the chair. Invite relaxation into your shoulders and neck. Roll your shoulders back and down and move your head from side to side. Relax through the forehead, the jaws, behind the eyes. Notice any sensations in the feet and hands—temperature, tingling, pulsing.* (Pause.) *Now take a few deep breaths, filling your belly like a balloon on the inhale, and then releasing and letting go on the exhale. Perhaps place your hands on your belly to witness this miracle of breath coming and going with each rise and fall.* (Pause for 1–2 minutes.)

If you notice any thoughts rising, like I'm not doing this right, *or* I'm not a good person—*any self-judgments, anxiety, or fear—relax them all on the exhale and offer yourself compassion. Maybe place your hand on your heart and remind yourself that you're okay just as you are.* (Pause.) *By practicing mindfulness and self-compassion, we're training in not going against ourselves, not judging or blaming ourselves for anything.* (Allow silence for the next few minutes or breaths, depending on the experience of participants; invite a student to ring the bell three times.) *Take a stretch, maybe a twist, and come back to the room and notice how you feel.*

Step 3: Debrief (partners, then whole class, 5–10 min.)

1. What's "alive" for you in this moment?
2. Of what body sensations were you aware?
3. Did you notice any judgments or challenging emotions arise? If so, did you offer yourself any kind gesture or words? What did you say?

Step 4: Read "Love After Love" (2 min.)

Read poem aloud. Encourage students to visualize what they hear.

Step 5: Making Connections (5–10 min.)

1. What do you appreciate about this poem?
2. What images or phrases stand out in your mind?
3. What is this poem saying to you?

Step 6: Cloze Listening Activity (Handout A) (10 min.)

Distribute the listening worksheet and, after reviewing unfamiliar vocabulary, read the poem a second time and have students fill in the missing words.

Step 7: Text-Dependent Questions (Handout B; Answers on Handout C) (15–20 min.)

Distribute Handout B for students to complete questions, either alone, with a partner, or in small groups.

Step 8: Text Response (Handout B; Sample Response on Handout C)

Prompt: Why do you think this poem is titled "Love After Love"? What is the poet's message about the importance of self-love?

Step 9: Self-Reflection (Handout B)

Prompt: Having gained some experience practicing mindfulness and self-compassion, can you identify a stressful moment when you paused and offered yourself some kindness? If not, when would you like to remember to do so in the future?

Step 10: Poem Writing (Handout D, E, or F) (10–15 min.)

Brainstorm

Small groups list positive emotions, their special place, ways to greet someone, things you say to make someone feel welcome, hurtful actions, their best qualities, and keepsakes.

Poem Writing

Distribute Handout D, E, or F, depending on students' fluency in English and creative writing experience.

Step 11: Prose Writing Option

Prompt: How do you "feast on your life"? Think of something you enjoy doing when you truly feel connected to yourself. What thoughts, feelings, and sensations arise in you? How does this activity nurture you?

TAKEAWAY

It's important to remember that it's not our fault for falling into forgetfulness. No blame needs to be assigned for failing to love ourselves fully just as we are. We only need to wake from the trance of self-judgment again and again by applying mindfulness and self-compassion.

EXTENSION

Spend some time gazing at your reflection in the mirror. Then write a love letter (or a desperate note) to yourself. Say everything you need to say. If the tone is harsh, that's okay. Simply allow whatever needs to be expressed to spill onto the page, remembering that thoughts are just thoughts and feelings are just feelings—they're not fact, and they're not permanent. Finally, appreciate all your efforts to train your mind, to be a witness to your experience, and to open your heart. What are some loving words you can share from your wisest, most compassionate self?

Love After Love
by Derek Walcott

The time will come
when, with elation,
you will greet yourself arriving
at your own door, in your own mirror,
5 and each will smile at the other's welcome,

and say, sit here. Eat.
You will love again the stranger who was your self.
Give wine. Give bread. Give back your heart
to itself, to the stranger who has loved you

10 all your life, whom you ignored
for another, who knows you by heart.
Take down the love letters from the bookshelf,

the photographs, the desperate notes,
peel your own image from the mirror.
15 Sit. Feast on your life.

Handout A

Cloze Listening Activity

Name: ______________________________

Listen to the poem and use the words to fill in the blanks.

desperate	mirror	smile	elation	stranger
ignored	arriving	peel	feast	

Love After Love
by Derek Walcott

The time will come
when, with (1) ____________________,
you will greet yourself (2) ____________________
at your own door, in your own (3) ____________________,
5 and each will (4) ____________________ at the other's welcome,
and say, sit here. Eat.
You will love again the (5) ____________________ who was your self.
Give wine. Give bread. Give back your heart
to itself, to the stranger who has loved you
10 all your life, whom you (6) ____________________
for another, who knows you by heart.
Take down the love letters from the bookshelf,
the photographs, the (7) ____________________ notes,
(8) ____________________ your own image from the mirror.
15 Sit. (9) ____________________ on your life.

Handout B

Text-Dependent Questions, Text Response, and Personal Reflection

Name: ______________________________

Text-Dependent Questions

1. Highlight eight concrete nouns in the poem. What mood do these objects evoke?

____

____

2. What does the word "elation" mean? Use context clues.

____

____

3. Find three examples of repetition in the poem.

____

____

4. What feeling does the repetition invoke? In other words, what is the poem's mood?

____

____

5. What can we guess (infer) from the poet's command to "peel your own image from the mirror"?

____

____

6. What's surprising (ironic) about Walcott referring to the person "who has loved you all your life" as "the stranger"?

____

____

Continued on next page

Text Response

Examine the theme of the poem and its development.

Prompt

Why do you think this poem is entitled "Love After Love"? What is the poet's message about the importance of self-love? What words does he use to convince us? Cite textual evidence.

____

____

____

____

____

____

Self-Reflection

Having gained some experience practicing mindfulness and self-compassion, can you identify a stressful moment when you paused and offered yourself some kindness? If not, when would you like to remember to do so in the future?

____

____

____

____

____

____

HANDOUT C

Handout C

Text-Dependent Questions Answer Key and Sample Text Response

Text-Dependent Questions Answer Key

1. Door, mirror, wine, bread, heart, love letters, bookshelf, photographs, notes; nurturing, romantic, nostalgic
2. great happiness
3. Your own door, your own mirror; give wine. give bread. give back your heart . . . the stranger who has loved you . . . whom you ignored . . . who knows you
4. *Answers will vary.* The insistent quality of the repetition sends a powerful message of the importance of loving oneself; confident, urgent
5. Know yourself intimately and accept yourself fully
6. A stranger is usually considered someone we have never met before. It may seem impossible to be a stranger to oneself.

Sample Text Response

Walcott titled this poem “Love After Love” because he is pointing out the fact that the most enduring relationship that we will have in our lifetime is with ourselves. We would do well to nurture and honor it. In lines 8–11, the poet commands us: “Give back your heart/to itself” the one “whom you ignored for another.” When we continually seek love outside ourselves, we risk losing touch with ourselves, our feelings, and our values, and we may become a stranger to ourselves. On the other hand, by turning our attention inward and becoming aware of our own thoughts, feelings, and sensations, seeing their impermanent nature, and offering ourselves kindness, we may develop the confidence to face our fears, challenge negative habitual patterns, and stand with ourselves for the rest of our lives.

Handout D

Basic Poem Writing Play Sheet

Name: ______________________________

Brainstorm 3–5 words in each category.

Positive Emotions	Special Places	Drinks	Favorite Foods

Continued on next page

HANDOUT D 2 / 2

Title: ____

(save the title for last and make it surprising or just right for your words)

The time will come

when, with ____________________
(positive emotion)

you will greet yourself arriving

at your own ____________________, in your own ____________________
(special place) *(special place)*

Give ____________________. Give ____________________. Give back your heart
(drink) *(food)*

to itself, to the stranger who has loved you all your life.

Draw a picture of your reunion with yourself.

Handout E

Intermediate Poem Writing Play Sheet

Name: ______________________________

Title: ____
(save the title for last and make it surprising or just right for your words)

The time will come

when, with ____________________
(positive emotion)

you will greet yourself arriving

at your own ____________________, in your own ____________________
(special place) *(special place)*

and each will ____________________ at the other's welcome,
(action verb)

and say, ________________________. ________________________
(things you say to make someone feel welcome)

You will love again the stranger who was your self.

Give ____________________. Give ____________________. Give back your heart
(drink) *(food)*

to itself, to the stranger who has loved you

all your life, whom you ____
(hurtful action)

for another, who knows ____
(one of your best qualities)

Take down the ____________________
(keepsake)

the ____________________, the ____________________
(keepsake) *(keepsake)*

____.
(command)

____.
(command)

HANDOUT E

Handout F

Advanced Poem Writing Play Sheet

Name: ______________________________

Use the following template as a guide to write your own version of the poem. Feel free to change it or abandon it at any point.

Title: ____

(save the title for last and make it surprising or just right for your words)

The time will come

when, with _______________________

you will greet yourself arriving

at your own _______________________, in your own _______________________

and each will _______________________ at the other's welcome,

and say, _______________________. _______________________

You will love again the stranger who was your self.

Give _______________________. Give _______________________. Give back your heart

to itself, to the stranger who has loved you

all your life, whom you ________________________________

for another, who knows ________________________________

Take down the ___________________________

the ___________________________, the ___________________________

____.

____.

CREATIVE WRITING EXAMPLES

Poetry

Love After Lust

The time will come when,
with contentment, you will greet yourself arriving
at your own backyard,
in your own field of sunflowers,
and each will cry at the other's welcome,
and say, "Pleasure to meet you! Come in!"
You will love again the stranger who was your self.
Give matcha. Give peaches.
Give back your heart to itself,
to the stranger who has loved you all your life,
whom you shoved
for another, who knows your devotion.
Take down the disposable pictures, the messages, the memories.
Feel the calmness after the storm.
Marinate in it.

—Sammi, eleventh grade

Prose

Moments in the garden. Listening. What is good to do next? Here I feel connected—connected to the ground. I'm intimately aware that the ground is the place of both birth and death—a lesson in impermanence, the full circle of life. A spectacular display of yellow spider dahlias here and the concentrated effort of a single bearded iris about to bloom over there. I don't know which is more beautiful. And the bright pink foxglove that's gone to seed (or I hope it's gone to seed) and will magically reappear in another season. Plants speak in a quieter language—one without words, and they accept me fully, just as I am.

—Laura Bean (author)

REFERENCES, RESOURCES, AND FURTHER READING

Bluth, Karen, and Kristin D. Neff. "New Frontiers in Understanding the Benefits of Self-Compassion." *Self and Identity.* 17, no. 6 (August 2018): 1–4. https://doi.org/10.1080/15298868.2018.1508494.

Kirschner, Hans, Willem Kuyken, Kim Wright, Henrietta Roberts, Claire Brejcha, and Anke Karl. "Soothing Your Heart and Feeling Connected: A New Experimental Paradigm to Study the Benefits of Self-Compassion." *Clinical Psychological Science* no. 7 (February 2019): 545–65.

Neff, K. D., and K. A. Dahm. "Self-Compassion: What It Is, What It Does, and How It Relates to Mindfulness." In *Handbook of Mindfulness and Self-Regulation*, edited by M. Robinson, B. Meier, and B. Ostafin, 121–37. New York: Springer, 2015.

Ruiz, Don Miguel. *The Four Agreements.* San Rafael: Amber-Allen, 1997.

Walcott, Derek. "Love After Love." Dunia Agit Law School. Video montage and poetry reading, 2:07. Uploaded August 12, 2020. www.youtube.com/watch?v=TSyP2OwHUIs (accessed August 1, 2022).

Lesson Nine

Noticing Habits

"Autobiography in Five Short Chapters"
by Portia Nelson

"How we spend our days is of course how we spend our lives."

~ Annie Dillard

OBJECTIVES

Mindfulness Skills	Explore physical sensations associated with fear, discomfort, triggering thoughts and feelings Identify a habitual pattern one would like to change
CASEL Competencies Highlight	Self-management: • Identify and use stress-management techniques • Set personal goals
Creative Writing Task (Aligns with CCSS.ELA-LITERACY.W.9-10.3 a-e; W.9-10.4-6; L.9-10.1 a,b; L.9-10.2 a-c; L.9-10.3 a; ELD Part I, C, 10, 12 and ELD Part II, A-C)	Compose a poem or personal narrative that demonstrates honest self-reflection tempered with self-compassion
Academic Writing Task (Aligns with CCSS.ELA-LITERACY.W.9-10.1; W.9-10.4-6; L.9-10.1 a, b; L.9-10.2 a-c; L.9-10.3 a; ELD Part I, C, 11, 12 and ELD Part II, A-C)	Analyze theme and its development in poem

INTRODUCTION

We live in an era of engineered addiction, hooking us on food, our cell phones, and social media, not to mention drugs and alcohol. Noticing what we do moment by moment, with kindness and curiosity, is a powerful antidote to this automaticity. By learning to lean into uncomfortable feelings that send us to the refrigerator or Facebook, we can wake ourselves up from living on autopilot and experience greater freedom.

The journey from mindlessness to mindfulness is the journey of a lifetime. Needless to say, we will encounter many setbacks along the way. In Portia Nelson's poem "Autobiography in Five Short Chapters," a precarious sidewalk with holes serves as a simple and powerful metaphor for the ease with which we fall into habitual tendencies. The good news is that each time we do, we gain more experience, as well as the power to make decisions that benefit both ourselves and our community. As the playwright Samuel Beckett advised: "Fail. Fail again. Fail better."

DID YOU KNOW? REWIRING REWARD-BASED LEARNING

Changing behavior is not easy. Even if we know intellectually that making a change will be good for us, when push comes to shove, we tend to fall back on old, familiar habits. This is because, in stressful situations, our prefrontal cortex, the most highly evolved, thinking part of our brain, goes offline, and the more primitive limbic system kicks in. In the limbic system, reward-based (pleasure-seeking) learning dominates; we repeat actions that gave us a boost, however fleeting, or those that provided momentary relief from challenging emotions, like sadness and anxiety.

The good news is that research has shown that practicing mindfulness, with its emphasis on turning toward our experience and becoming curious about it, can help us make real change. By learning to tolerate unpleasant emotions and cravings and observing how they show up in our bodies, such as a pounding chest, tightness, or restlessness, we can halt reactive habit patterns and create new ones grounded in awareness. Rather than relying on extrinsic rewards, such as a sugar rush from a piece of chocolate cake or the number on a bathroom scale, we may experience the intrinsic reward of healthy eating and self-compassion.

STUDENT LESSON OBJECTIVES

- ✔ Practice observing thoughts and emotions that arise during mindfulness practice, particularly self-judgments, and offer yourself compassion
- ✔ Experiment with calling to mind something you crave and becoming curious about the effects on your body
- ✔ Identify a habitual pattern you would like to change
- ✔ Do a close reading of the poem "Autobiography in Five Short Chapters" by Portia Nelson and answer questions about it
- ✔ Write your own version of the poem or a story inspired by it
- ✔ Write a paragraph sharing what you think the poet's message is and refer to lines from the poem to show it

Step 1: Quick Write (5 min.) and Partner Share (5 min.)

Options

1. ***Prompt:*** What habits do you have that you would you like to strengthen? weaken?
2. ***Prompt:*** Write about a time when you did something differently from the way you usually do it. It could be stepping outside of your comfort zone in class, sports, or in a relationship. What did you do differently, and what was the result?

Step 2: Guided Practice (5–7 min.)

Teacher Note: The following guided practice is adapted from a script by psychiatrist and neuroscientist Dr. Judson Brewer. It invites students to explore how cravings arise in the mind and body so they may free themselves from them.

Script

First, find a comfortable position and drop into the body, moving your head from side to side, releasing any tension in the neck, maybe dropping an ear to one shoulder without raising the shoulder to meet it . . . and then the other. Just check in with the body and be curious—what's alive for you right now? Allow any tension to melt, as if you were being bathed in a warm, relaxing shower.

Listen to the bell. (Ring bell.) *Now turn your attention to the waves of breath coming and going, your chest rising with the inhalation and falling with the exhalation. Just enjoy this natural rhythm of the breath, without needing to do anything. Just inhale . . . and exhale. Deep . . . and slow.*

Today we're going to play with exploring our cravings and seeing how they show up in our bodies. So, call to mind something you love, maybe it's your go-to food when you're stressed, or something that feels like an itch you have to scratch—maybe it's checking your Instagram feed. It could be something pleasant or something unpleasant you feel you have to deal with.

When you've got something in mind, begin to notice what this urge feels like in your body—this grasping after something pleasant or pushing away what's unpleasant. Just get curious and notice where it shows up in your body. And as you bring this kind curiosity to your experience, notice what happens. Does the sensation change? Does it become stronger or begin to fade?

Now just rest in your body, noticing what it feels like to bring awareness to cravings. And stay curious about other urges that may pop up—future fantasies or habits of beating yourself up over something you said or did in the past. Just identify what sensations arise in the body and hold each one with kindness and curiosity. (Ring bell.)

Step 3: Debrief (partners, then whole class, 5–10 min.)

(Optional, given the sensitive nature of this practice.)

1. Could you bring something to mind that you crave or tend to do automatically without thinking?
2. Where in your body did you notice the impulse to act? What did it feel like?
3. Did you notice any change as you stayed with the sensation?

Step 4: Read "Autobiography in Five Short Chapters" (2 min.)

Read poem aloud. Encourage students to visualize what they hear.

Step 5: Making Connections (5–10 min.)

1. What do you like about this poem?
2. What words or phrases do you remember?
3. What is this poem saying to you?

Step 6: Cloze Listening Activity (Handout A) (10 min.)

Distribute the listening worksheet and, after reviewing unfamiliar vocabulary words, read poem a second time and have students fill in the missing words.

Step 7: Text-Dependent Questions (Handout B; Answers on Handout C) (15–20 min.)

Distribute Handout B for students to complete questions, either alone, with a partner, or in small groups.

Step 8: Text Response (Handout B; Sample Response on Handout C)

Prompt: Why do you think this poem is titled "An Autobiography in Five Short Chapters"? What is the poet's message (theme)? How does the use of repetition highlight the theme?

Step 9: Self-Reflection (Handout B)

Prompt: What is a "hole" into which you repeatedly fall? How does it impact your life?

Step 10: Poem Writing (Handout D, E, or F) (10–15 min.)

Distribute Handout D, E, or F, depending on students' fluency in English and creative writing experience.

Step 11: Prose Writing Option

Prompt: Write about a time when you met a challenge by observing your thoughts, feelings, and sensations, and applying intentional effort.

TAKEAWAY

Training ourselves to slow down and get curious about our experience allows us to step off the treadmill of habitual patterns. By shining the light of our loving awareness on our habits and offering ourselves compassion, we can change and grow.

EXTENSION

In the poem "If You Would Grow, Shed the Light of Self-Awareness on Yourself" by Daniel F. Mead, the speaker encourages us to be patient and kind with ourselves as we move toward change—"be patient, not demanding/accepting, not condemning, . . . a flower cannot be opened with a hammer." Ask students to reflect upon the most important attributes they would like to cultivate and see blossom in themselves.

Autobiography in Five Short Chapters
by Portia Nelson

Chapter I
I walk down the street.
There is a deep hole in the sidewalk.
I fall in.
I am lost . . . I am helpless.
5 It isn't my fault.
It takes me forever to find a way out.

Chapter II
I walk down the same street.
There is a deep hole in the sidewalk.
I pretend I don't see it.
10 I fall in again.
I can't believe I am in the same place.
But it isn't my fault.
It still takes a long time to get out.

Chapter III
I walk down the same street.
15 There is a deep hole in the sidewalk.
I see it is there.
I still fall in . . . it's a habit.
My eyes are open.
I know where I am.
20 It is *my* fault.
I get out immediately.

Chapter IV
I walk down the same street.
There is a deep hole in the sidewalk.
I walk around it.

Chapter V
25 I walk down another street.

Handout A

Cloze Listening Activity

Name: ______________________________

Listen to the poem and use the words to fill in the blanks.

another	fault	habit	believe
around	helpless	immediately	pretend

Autobiography in Five Short Chapters
by Portia Nelson

Chapter I

I walk down the street.

There is a deep hole in the sidewalk.

I fall in.

I am lost . . . I am (1) ___________________.

5 It isn't my fault.

It takes me forever to find a way out.

Chapter II

I walk down the same street.

There is a deep hole in the sidewalk.

I (2) ___________________ I don't see it.

10 I fall in again.

I can't (3) ___________________ I am in the same place.

But it isn't my fault.

It still takes a long time to get out.

Chapter III

I walk down the same street.

15 There is a deep hole in the sidewalk.

I see it is there.

I still fall in . . . it's a (4) ___________________.

Continued on next page

HANDOUT A 2 / 2

My eyes are open.

I know where I am.

20 It is *my* (5) _________________.

I get out (6) _________________.

Chapter IV

I walk down the same street.

There is a deep hole in the sidewalk.

I walk (7) _________________ it.

Chapter V

25 I walk down (8) _________________ street.

Handout B

Text-Dependent Questions, Text Response, and Personal Reflection

Name: ______________________________

Text-Dependent Questions

1. After falling in the hole the first time, the speaker says, "I am lost . . . I am helpless./It isn't my fault" (lines 4–5). How much personal power (agency) do they feel they have? What do they see themselves as?

____

____

2. What does the hole in the sidewalk represent (symbolize)?

____

____

3. In chapter 3, the speaker admits that falling into the hole is a habit. How does this awareness change the way the speaker sees themselves? Cite textual evidence.

____

____

4. What does this allow the speaker to do?

____

____

5. Making real change requires awareness. What other character traits does the speaker demonstrate?

____

____

6. In chapter 5, the speaker says, "I walk down another street." What can we guess (infer) from this line?

____

____

Continued on next page

Text Response

Examine the theme and its development in the poem.

Prompt

Why do you think this poem is titled "An Autobiography in Five Short Chapters"? What is the poet's message (theme)? How does the use of repetition highlight the theme? Include lines from the poem that show (illustrate) it.

Self-Reflection

What is a "hole" into which you repeatedly fall? How does it impact your life?

Handout C

Text-Dependent Questions Answer Key and Sample Text Response

Text-Dependent Questions Answer Key

1. very little; they see themselves as a blameless victim of circumstance
2. habitual patterns that don't serve the person
3. They recognize a pattern that no longer serves them and accept responsibility for it rather than seeing themselves as a victim; "it's a habit./My eyes are open . . ./It is *my* fault."
4. They can quickly extract themselves from the hole (make a meaningful change in their life).
5. self-honesty and the courage to examine unhealthy patterns in their life
6. *Answers will vary*. They no longer place themselves in situations which will tempt them to repeat unhealthy repetitive patterns; they are forming new ways of thinking and approaching situations.

Sample Text Response

Perhaps the poem is titled "An Autobiography in Five Short Chapters" because it is talking about making a change in one's life. This journey to overcome habitual patterns requires patience and perseverance, and is anything but short, so there's some irony in the title as well—"I fall in again" (line 10), "I still fall in . . . it's a habit" (line 17). The repetitive quality of the poem mimics our habitual tendencies on the journey to become more aware and freer.

HANDOUT C

Handout D

Basic Poem Writing Play Sheet

Name: ______________________________

Directions: Draw pictures in each square below and complete the sentence starters.

Picture 1: What is something you often do that you would like to do differently?

Picture 2: What positive thing does this experience remind you of from the past?

Picture 3: What do you notice when you do it now? What effect does it have?

Picture 4: How do you want to change your behavior?

What I Do	What I Remember

What I Notice	What I Want to Do Differently

Continued on next page

One habit I want to change is ______________________________________.
(habit)

It reminds me of ______________________________________.
(good memory)

When I ______________________, I ______________________________________.
(habit) *(what do you notice? how do you feel)?*

In the future I want to ______________________________________.
(new habit)

Example

One habit I want to change is eating Synder's Sourdough Hard Pretzels.

They remind me of my childhood, playing cards with my dad, my eldest brother, and my grandma at a card table in the living room.

When I eat them, I get acid indigestion.

In the future, I want to make a salad instead.

Handout E

Intermediate Poem Writing Play Sheet

Name: ______________________________

Brainstorm three to five words for each category below.

Places You Often Go	Who or What You See There	What You Do or Say	What You Wish to Do Differently

Continued on next page

Now, think of a "hole" into which you repeatedly fall. Play with the use of repetition to write your own "autobiography" in five short chapters, showing what you've learned from being curious about your repetitive patterns and how you might act differently in the future.

Title: ______________________________

(save the title for last and make it surprising or just right for your words)

Chapter I

I walk ______________________
(place)

There is ______________________________
(Who or what do you see?) (line 2)

I ______________________________
(What do you do or say?) (line 3)

It isn't my fault. It takes me forever to find my way out.

Chapter II

I walk ______________________
(place)

There is ______________________________
(copy line 2)

I ______________________________
(copy line 3)

I can't believe I am in the same place again, but it isn't my fault.

It still takes me a long time to get out.

Chapter III

I walk ______________________
(place)

There is ______________________________
(copy line 2)

I ______________________________
(copy line 3)

Continued on next page

It's a habit.

It is my fault.

I get out immediately.

Chapter IV

I walk ____________________________

(place)

There is ____

(copy line 2)

I ____

(What do you do differently?)

Chapter V

I ____.

(What do you do differently?)

Handout F

Advanced Poem Writing Play Sheet

Name: ______________________________

Use the following template as a guide to write your own version of the poem. Feel free to change it or abandon it at any point.

Title: ____

(save the title for last and make it surprising or just right for your words)

Chapter I

I walk __________________________

There is ____

I ____

It isn't my fault. It takes me forever to find my way out.

Chapter II

I walk __________________________

There is ____

I ____

I can't believe I am in the same place again, but it isn't my fault.

It still takes me a long time to get out.

Chapter III

I walk __________________________

There is ____

I ____

It's a habit.

It is my fault.

I get out immediately.

Chapter IV

I walk __________________________

There is ____

I ____

Chapter V

I ____.

CREATIVE WRITING EXAMPLES

Poetry

Chip Problem

1 I walk down Third Avenue.
There is a smoke shop.
I go in and buy Hot Cheetos.
It isn't my fault. It takes me forever to find my way out.

2 I walk down the same street.
There is the same smoke shop.
I pretend I don't see it. Then I go in and buy chips.
I can't believe I am in the same place again, but it isn't my fault.
It still takes me a long time to get out.

3 I walk down the street
There is the same smoke shop.
I see it is there.
I go in again and buy chips.
It's a habit.
It is my fault.
I get out immediately.

4 I walk the same street.
There is the smoke shop on the street.
I walk past it.

5 I walk down another street.

—Antonio V., seventh grade, English learner

Friend Group

Chapter I
I walk into the wrong group of people.
There are people who will not help me.
I feel like there is nobody there for me.
It isn't my fault. It takes me forever to find my way out.

Chapter II
I walk into the same group of people.
There are people who put down others.
I watch in disappointment.
I can't believe I am in the same place again, but it isn't my fault.
It still takes me a long time to get out.

Chapter III
I walk with the same people.
There they go again putting people down.
I don't know what to do but just watch.
It's a habit.
It is my fault.
I get out immediately.

Chapter IV
I walk to another group of friends.
These are friends I can call "family."
I appreciate them.

Chapter V
I changed because of the people around me.

—Tristan, ninth grade

Tunneled Thoughts

Chapter I
I walk around in my thoughts.
There are tunnels leading me to people from my past, haunting me.
I say leave me alone, please.
It isn't my fault.
It takes me forever to find my way out.

Chapter II
I walk around in my thoughts.
There are tunnels leading me to people from my past, haunting me.
I say leave me alone, please.
I can't believe I am in the same hurtful place again, but it isn't my fault.
It still takes me a long time to get out.

Chapter III
I walk around in my thoughts.
There are tunnels leading me to people from my past, haunting me.
I say leave me alone, please.
It's a habit.
It is my fault for responding.
I get out immediately.

Chapter IV
I walk around in my thoughts.
There are tunnels leading me to people from my past, haunting me.
I grew up and moved on from the manipulative mind games.

Chapter V
I'm cautious and stopped going into the tunnels leading me to people from my past.

—Sammi, eleventh grade

Pit of My Stomach

I walk into my head.
This is my greatest fear.
I hear what sounds like gibberish.
It isn't my fault. It takes me forever to find my way out.

I walk into my hands.
There is an eruption.
I try to conceal it.
I can't believe I am in the same place again, but it isn't my fault.
It still takes me a long time to get out.

I walk into my eyes.
There are eyes everywhere.
I go blurry.
It's a habit.
It is my fault.
I get out immediately.

I walk into my head.
There is my greatest fear.
I greet my greatest fear. It says, "Hello."
I ask why I feel this way. It answers with a hug.

—Maddy, twelfth grade

Prose

How I Got My Ten-Year-Old Job

It was a normal day, and I was playing with my dog when my mom said, "Hey Marcos, would you like to go with me to the mall?" "Okay," I said, "let me go put on my shoes."

When we got there, I asked her, "Can I go to Game Stop?" She said, "Okay, just don't get lost."

At the store, they were putting out a sign for the new World War II game. I was so happy. I ran back to her and asked, "Can I please have that game?" "What game?" she asked. "The new game that came out." "Okay. Let's go see."

As soon as she saw it, she said no. It cost sixty dollars. I pleaded, "Then, can you get it for me for Christmas?" "Christmas is in five months!" she shot back. "If you want it, get a job to buy it because things here are not free. You have to work for them."

The next day, coming back from school, I saw my neighbor cutting her grass. I said to myself, "I'm going to ask her for a job." I went up to her and said, "Mrs. Rivera, I'm wondering if you need someone to cut your grass?" She said, "Yes, I do need you to help me put some books in my car, okay?" When we finished, she gave me enough money to buy my video game.

—Marcos, seventh grade, English learner

REFERENCES, RESOURCES, AND FURTHER READING

Brewer, Judson. "A Simple Way to Break a Bad Habit." Filmed November 2015. TEDMED video, 9:25. www.youtube.com/watch?v=-moW9jvvMr4 (accessed September 29, 2022). https://drjud.com/wp-content/uploads/2021/03/Unwinding-Anxiety-Habit-Mapper-from-DrJud-1-1.pdf (accessed August 1, 2022).

Brewer, Judson A., Andrea Ruf, Ariel L. Beccia, Gloria I. Essien, Leonard M. Finn, Remko van Lutterveld, and Ashley E. Mason. "Can Mindfulness Address Maladaptive Eating Behaviors? Why Traditional Diet Plans Fail and How New Mechanistic Insights May Lead to Novel Interventions." *Frontiers in Psychology* 9 (September 2018): 1–11.

Mead, Daniel F. "If You Would Grow, Shed the Light of Self-Awareness on Yourself." August 12, 2016. https://themindfulbrain.net/mindful-poetry-day-8 (accessed August 6, 2022).

Nelson, Portia. "Autobiography in Five Short Chapters." YouTube video, 1:16. August 15, 2009. www.youtube.com/watch?v=jSCA0EWR2RE (accessed August 1, 2022).

Lesson Ten

Empathy and Compassion

"Saint Francis and the Sow" by Galway Kinnell

"Real empathy is sometimes not insisting that it will be okay but acknowledging that it is not."

~ Sheryl Sandberg

OBJECTIVES

Mindfulness Skills	Visualize fountain in heart Practice perspective-taking Offer another person empathy and compassion
CASEL Competencies Highlight	Social awareness: • Take others' perspective • Demonstrate empathy and compassion
Creative Writing Task (Aligns with CCSS.ELA-LITERACY.W.9-10.3 a-e, W.9-10.4-6; L.9-10.1 a,b; L.9-10.2 a-c; L.9-10.3 a; ELD Part I, C, 10, 12 and ELD Part II, A-C)	Produce a poem or letter offering compassionate care to an animal, yourself, or another person
Academic Writing Task (Aligns with CCSS.ELA-LITERACY.W.9-10.1; W.9-10.4-6, L.9-10.1 a, b; L.9-10.2 a-c; L.9-10.3 a; ELD Part I, C, 11, 12 and ELD Part II, A-C)	Analyze theme and its development in poem

INTRODUCTION

It's easy "to other." This lesson is dedicated to breaking down the barriers we subconsciously erect between ourselves and those we perceive to be different from us. To look for beauty and connection, where what feels most comfortable is to dismiss or reject, is to work with deep-seated habits of mind.

This generosity of spirit is much needed in today's world, with the explosion of social media forcing young people to manage their own publicity and marketing campaigns beginning in the second or third grade. Teaching and modeling empathy and compassion to mitigate pervasive cyberbullying is paramount.

"Saint Francis and the Sow" reminds students to see beauty where it might be easy to overlook it. The mention of "fourteen teats and fourteen mouths sucking and blowing" may result in a few giggles and a classroom full of warm hearts as students write to "reteach a thing its loveliness."

DID YOU KNOW? THE VALUE OF EMPATHY

We are hard-wired for kindness and empathy. When we see someone suffering, our natural inclination (and our neurobiology) is to feel their pain, as well. This is due to mirror neurons, whose job is to track the emotions, physical movements, and intentions of whomever we are with and reproduce the sensed state in our own brains. In the case of witnessing someone's pain, the pain receptors in our own brains light up, though to a lesser degree. This phenomenon is called emotional resonance or emotional contagion.

Whether we choose to see someone's suffering as a disease we can catch, or a profound human experience that we have the privilege of sharing, depends on our perspective. Psychiatrist and researcher Helen Riess, author of *The Empathy Effect*, conducted research on how empathy affects physicians' well-being. She found that when doctors chose to stay open and attentive to the emotional lives of their patients and acknowledged their own feelings of emotional resonance, both they and their patients benefited. Patients were more trusting and cooperative, and doctors felt more connected and suffered less from compassion fatigue.

However, it can be easy to become overwhelmed by another's suffering. Fortunately, true empathy involves a cognitive component, as well. Not only do we feel what others feel, but we are also able to imagine ourselves in their shoes. Practicing perspective-taking helps us to separate our pain from theirs and is the most sustainable way to build empathetic concern or compassion.

As teachers, therapists, and social workers, we're also subject to compassion fatigue. Practicing mindfulness adds a protective layer, or "shield," so we don't take on others' emotions so deeply that they affect us adversely. We're better able to self-regulate and stay open to the wide range of emotions students express. We remain curious, ask questions, and listen to their answers without attempting to shut them down or fix them. This normalizes students' emotions and helps them to clarify what they're feeling so we may respond in a way that is helpful. We're also modeling how to be more sensitive to others' feelings.

STUDENT LESSON OBJECTIVES

- ✔ Picture a fountain of love in your heart
- ✔ Practice putting yourself in someone else's shoes and wishing them well
- ✔ Do a close reading of the poem "St. Francis and the Sow" by Galway Kinnell and answer questions about it
- ✔ Write your own version of the poem or a story inspired by it
- ✔ Write a paragraph sharing what you think the poet's message is and prove it with lines from the poem

Step 1: Quick Write (5 min.) and Partner Share (5 min.)

Option 1

Prompt: Think of a time you comforted someone who was going through a rough patch. What was the situation? What did you say or do?

Option 2

Prompt: Make a list of animals, people, and/or parts of the natural world that are suffering.

Step 2: Guided Practice (5–7 min.)

Teacher Note: Mindfulness encourages young people to continue to turn their attention inward. At this point in the course, they may be becoming more aware of the voice of the inner critic and the rapidity with which they externalize this painful experience by judging others. This lesson includes a brief guided visualization of offering themselves self-compassion and extending it to others who are in need of the healing waters of compassion.

Script

Taking a moment to pause and turn our attention inward can be a scary act. Sometimes our inner worlds can feel like washing machines on the spin cycle. (Pause.) *We may feel afraid that if we stop to take a look, we'll go crazy with all the churning thoughts and emotions, all the stories of our faults and limitations. So, we should acknowledge the courage it takes to pause from our constant doing to practice simply being with ourselves, just as we are, without the need to change anything . . . and offer ourselves kindness. Remember that this is a safe place to just be, and that just like you, everyone around you is also subject to their own negative self-talk, to their judgments and self-criticisms.* (Pause; then ring bell.)

Beginning with some gentle stretches, settle into the body, softening your belly. (Pause while students settle themselves.) *Imagine a string extending from the top of your head, raising your spine toward the ceiling, and dropping your shoulders toward the floor. Find the breath in your body, in your chest and your belly. And take a few slow, deep breaths.*

Now tune into your mind's eye, imagining a fountain in your heart center, flowing with an effervescent, golden-colored nectar. Imagine this nectar streaming through your chest and shoulders, down your arms, all the way to your fingertips . . . and cascading into your belly, pelvis, and hips, then down through your legs all the way to the tips of your toes. (Pause.) *And as it flows, feel any places of holding in your body begin to melt, any disturbing thoughts or storylines dissolving in the radiance of this golden light.*

And as it flows, imagine this golden nectar extending beyond the limits of your own body, showering someone you know who needs love and self-acceptance at this moment. Imagine them being bathed in these healing waters and smiling at you with love and gratitude for your caring concern. (Invite a student to ring the bell.) *Wiggle your fingers and toes, and when you're ready, open your eyes. And take a moment to notice how you feel.*

Step 3: Debrief (partners, then whole class, 5–10 min.)

1. How do you feel?
2. Were you able to imagine a fountain in your heart? What was it like?
3. Did you share the golden nectar with someone else? With whom?

Step 4: Read "Saint Francis and the Sow" (2 min.)

Read poem aloud. Encourage students to visualize what they hear.

Step 5: Making Connections (5–10 min.)

1. What do you appreciate about this poem?
2. What words or phrases do you remember?
3. What images stand out in your mind?

Step 6: Cloze Listening Activity (Handout A) (10 min.)

Distribute the listening worksheet and, after reviewing unfamiliar vocabulary words, read the poem a second time and have students fill in the missing words.

Step 7: Text-Dependent Questions (Handout B; Answers on Handout C) (10–15 min.)

Distribute Handout B for students to complete questions, either alone, with a partner, or in small groups.

Step 8: Text Response (Handout B; Sample Response on Handout C)

Prompt: In the poem, Kinnell paints a detailed portrait in the words of a mother pig reflecting on her self-worth. What message do you think he's trying to convey?

Step 9: Self-Reflection (Handout B)

Prompt: How does showing compassion make the world a better place? Give an example from your life.

Step 10: Poem Writing (Handout D, E, or F) (10–15 min.)

Distribute Handout D, E, or F, depending on students' fluency in English and creative writing experience.

Step 11: Prose Writing Option

Prompt: Write a letter of encouragement and support to someone or something that is suffering—an animal, a part of nature, someone who may have come to mind in your quick write, or perhaps yourself. As inspiration, you may like to start with the following line from the poem: "Sometimes it is necessary to reteach a thing its loveliness."

TAKEAWAY

Self-compassion and empathy are intricately linked. It's impossible to give to others what we ourselves don't have. Gaining perspective on our own minds and offering ourselves unconditional love is a prerequisite to showing up for others in an effective and compassionate way.

EXTENSION

Ask students to brainstorm a list of positive messages they could offer to themselves or to someone in need of a boost. Example phrases include: *You are worthwhile. You are beautiful all the way deep in your heart. You are shy, and that's okay. You are brave. You do matter. You have lots of feelings, and they are important. You deserve to have your needs met. You have lots of laughter deep inside. I love you. I am so proud of you.* These messages could be used to create a "Compliments" flyer with personalized messages at the bottom, which students could tear off.

Saint Francis and the Sow
by Galway Kinnell

The bud
stands for all things,
even for those things that don't flower,
for everything flowers, from within, of self-blessing;
5 though sometimes it is necessary
to reteach a thing its loveliness,
to put a hand on the brow
of the flower
and retell it in words and in touch
10 it is lovely
until it flowers again from within, of self-blessing;
as Saint Francis
put his hand on the creased forehead
of the sow, and told her in words and in touch
15 blessings of earth on the sow, and the sow
began remembering all down her thick length,
from the earthen snout all the way
through the fodder and slops to the spiritual curl of the tail,
from the hard spininess spiked out from the spine
20 down through the great broken heart
to the sheer blue milken dreaminess spurting and shuddering
from the fourteen teats into the fourteen mouths sucking and blowing beneath them:
the long, perfect loveliness of sow.

Handout A

Cloze Listening Activity

Name: ______________________________

Listen to the poem and use the words to fill in the blanks.

creased	blessings	touch	remembering	spininess
retell	reteach	self-blessing	brow	flower
snout	spiritual	broken	spurting	shuddering

Saint Francis and the Sow
by Galway Kinnell

The bud
stands for all things,
even for those things that don't (1) ________________,
for everything flowers, from within, of (2) ________________;
5 though sometimes it is necessary
to (3) ________________ a thing its loveliness,
to put a hand on the (4) ________________
of the flower
and (5) ________________ it in words and in touch
10 it is lovely
until it flowers again from within, of self-blessing;
as Saint Francis
put his hand on the (6) ________________ forehead
of the sow, and told her in words and in (7) ________________
15 (8) ________________ of earth on the sow, and the sow
began (9) ________________ all down her thick length,
from the earthen (10) ________________ all the way
through the fodder and slops to the (11) ________________ curl of the tail,
from the hard (12) ________________ spiked out from the spine
20 down through the great (13) ________________ heart
to the sheer blue milken dreaminess (14) ______________ and (15) ______________
from the fourteen teats into the fourteen mouths sucking and blowing beneath them:
the long, perfect loveliness of sow.

Handout B

Text-Dependent Questions, Text Response, and Personal Reflection

Name: ______________________________

Text-Dependent Questions

1. Highlight ten concrete nouns from the poem.

____

____

2. In line 11, the poet writes about comforting a flower "until it flowers again from within, of self-blessing." What does "self-blessing" mean? Use context clues.

____

____

3. The poem is titled "Saint Francis and the Sow." Saint Francis was famous for showing great compassion to the animal world. Why do you think the poet chose a female pig (sow) as a subject for his poem?

____

____

4. What physical gesture does the speaker in the poem make to comfort the pig?

____

____

5. The poem opens with the line, "The bud stands for all things." What do you think the bud represents (symbolizes)?

____

____

6. "Spiritual curl" is a noun phrase (noun + adjective) that evokes a mystical feeling. Find one more.

____

____

Continued on next page

Text Response

Examine the theme and its development in the poem.

Prompt

In the poem, Kinnell paints a detailed portrait in the words of a mother pig reflecting on her self-worth. What message (theme) do you think he's trying to convey? What lines from the poem demonstrate it? Cite textual evidence.

____

____

____

____

____

____

Self-Reflection

How does showing compassion make the world a better place? Give an example from your life.

____

____

____

____

____

____

HANDOUT C

Handout C

Text-Dependent Questions Answer Key and Sample Text Response

Text-Dependent Questions Answer Key

1. bud, hand, brow, flower, forehead, sow, snout, tail, spine, heart, teats, mouths
2. to wish oneself well and to practice self-love
3. Pigs are generally considered to be dirty animals that wallow in the mud. The poet is challenging this bias by elevating the pig to a spiritual dimension.
4. They put their hand on her forehead and remind her that she is lovely
5. *Answers will vary.* The bud represents everyone's potential to love themselves completely and move through the world with confidence and grace; we can choose to bloom like a flower or stay a bud; the heart; the start of life.
6. "great broken heart"; "sheer blue milken dreaminess"

Sample Text Response

The theme of the poem "Saint Francis and the Sow" is empathy and compassion. Kinnell is calling our attention to an animal that isn't held in high regard. In the world of his poem, we are invited to look more closely and admire and empathize with the pig nursing her piglets. She is personified as reflecting on and "remembering" her worth, and as having a "great broken heart," something to which many of us can relate.

Handout D

Basic Poem Writing Play Sheet

Name: ______________________________

Copy your favorite line from the poem "Saint Francis and the Sow."

____

Next, brainstorm three to five words in each category below:

Animals that most people don't like	Unique part of their body	Descriptive adjectives

Now fill in the blanks with your ideas.

Sometimes it is necessary to reteach a thing its loveliness.

To put a hand on ________________________ *(part of the body)* of the ________________________ *(animal)*

And retell her in words and in touch

She is ________________________. *(adjective)*

Continued on next page

Draw a picture of your act of kindness.

Handout E

Intermediate Poem Writing Play Sheet

Name: ______________________________

Brainstorm words in the following categories, and then use your ideas to write your own version of the poem, offering compassionate care to an animal that is misunderstood, disdained, feared, or in danger.

Animal	Unique or signature part of its body	Descriptive adjectives

Continued on next page

HANDOUT E 2/2

Title: ____

(save this for last and make it surprising or just right for your poem)

Sometimes it is necessary

to reteach a thing its loveliness,

to put a hand on the ______________________ ______________________
(adjective) *(part of body)*

of the ______________________
(animal)

and retell them in words and in touch

They are ______________________.
(adjective)

and the ______________________ began remembering
(animal)

all down their ______________________ body
(adjective)

from the ______________________,
(part of body)

all the way down through ______________________________;
(a "distant" part of its body)

blessings of ______________________ on the ______________________
(something from nature) *(animal)*

May they remember their ______________________
(positive quality—noun)

the ________________, ________________ __________________ of ________________.
(adjective) *(adjective)* *(positive quality—noun)* *(animal)*

Handout F

Advanced Poem Writing Play Sheet

Name: ____________________________

Use the following template as a guide to write your own version of the poem. Feel free to change it or abandon it at any point.

Title: ____

(save this for last and make it surprising or just right for your poem)

Sometimes it is necessary

to reteach a thing its loveliness,

to put a hand on the _______________________

of the _______________________

and retell _______________________ in words and in touch

_______________________ is _______________________.

and the _______________________ began remembering

all down _______________________ body

from the _______________________,

all the way down through _______________________;

blessings of _______________________ on the _______________________

May ___________________ remember _____________________ _____________________

the ____________, _________________ __________________ of __________________.

CREATIVE WRITING EXAMPLES

Poetry

The Rat

Sometimes it is necessary
to reteach a thing its loveliness.
to put a finger on the translucent pink ears
of the rat
and retell it in words and in touch
it is adorable.

And the rat began remembering
all down its body
from the sensitive snout,
down through the muscular tail;
blessings of moonlight on the rat

May it remember its intelligence—
the friendly, pure, resourcefulness of rat.

—Austin, ninth grade

A Magical Life

Sometimes it is necessary
to reteach a thing its loveliness.
to put a hand on the cheek
of the girl
and retell her in words and in touch
she's thinking too much.

And the girl began remembering
all down her body,
from the top of her head
all down her legs to the bottom of her feet,
blessings of the water from the ocean on the girl
May she remember her kindness.

The magical, fearless loveliness of girl.

—Samantha, ninth grade

Journal Writing

Teacher Note: This journal writing sample and the poem that follows demonstrate how to revise a piece of free writing to create a new version of the poem without strictly following the poem writing template.

Sometimes it is necessary to reteach a thing its loveliness. I am lovely just as I am. I accept myself just as I am. All this is me. All this is my own perfect loveliness, from the kinky hair on the top of my head, all down the length of this roundish belly and wide hips, eyes that blink away the tears of a love who went away, to see the page I'm writing on. Blessings of earth and sky, blessings of all the creatures on this earth—the plants and animals, and the rain. All that is good and wholesome. All that is protective. Blessings! Blessings! May I remember! May I remember I have a right to be here and to be happy. May I cut through the craving to be small, the old energy that wants to forget who I am, that wants to live in a world of pain and suffering. Remembering our goodness. Remembering our connectedness. The natural goodness of ourselves just as we are. We're perfect just as we are. Blessings on us—a shower of blessings on us!

—Laura Bean (author)

Sometimes it is necessary to reteach a thing its loveliness.
To put a hand on the forehead of someone who is sick
and retell her in words and in touch
she is worthy.
And the girl began remembering
all down her feverish body
from the kinky hair on the top of her head,
all down the length of her roundish belly and wide hips,
eyes that blink away the tears of a love that went away.
Blessings of earth and sky,
of all the creatures on this earth,
the plants and animals and the rain.
All that is good and wholesome.
All that is protective.
May we remember our natural goodness, just as we are.
Blessings on us!
A shower of blessings on us!

—Laura Bean (author)

REFERENCES, RESOURCES, AND FURTHER READING

Brown, Brené. "The Power of Empathy—Dr. Brene Brown on empathy versus sympathy." Dailymotion.com. Animated educational video, 2:53. Uploaded October 26, 2014. www.dailymotion.com/video/x28nj7a (accessed August 1, 2022).

Kinnell, Galway. "Saint Francis and the Sow." Academy of American Poets. Video of poetry reading, 1:52. Uploaded May 19, 2017. www.youtube.com/watch?v=yBJ3Llp_Lj8 (accessed August 1, 2022).

Riess, Helen. "The Power of Empathy: Helen Riess at TEDxMiddlebury." Lecture, 17:02. Uploaded December 12, 2013. www.youtube.com/watch?v=baHrcC8B4WM (accessed August 1, 2022).

Riess, Helen, and Liz Neporent. *The Empathy Effect.* Boulder: Sounds True, 2018.

Riess, H., J. M. Kelley, R. W. Bailey, E. J. Dunn, and M. Phillips. "Empathy Training for Resident Physicians: A Randomized Controlled Trial of a Neuroscience-Informed Curriculum." *Journal of General Internal Medicine* 27, no. 10 (October 2012): 1280–86.

Suttie, Jill. "Why the World Needs an Empathy Revolution." Last modified February 1, 2019. https://greatergood.berkeley.edu/article/%E2%80%8Bitem/why_the_world_needs_an_empathy_revolution (accessed August 6, 2022).

Lesson Eleven

Forgiveness

"Revenge" by Taha Muhammad Ali

"Forgiveness means giving up all hope for a better past."

~ Lily Tomlin

OBJECTIVES

Mindfulness Skills	Investigate the power of forgiveness to free oneself from suffering and improve relationship skills Practice offering loving-kindness to self and others
CASEL Competencies Highlights	Social awareness: take others' perspectives, demonstrate empathy and compassion Relationship skills: resolve conflicts constructively
Creative Writing Task (Aligns with CCSS.ELA-LITERACY.W.9-10.3 a-e; W.9-10.4-6; L.9-10.1 a,b; L.9-10.2 a-c; L.9-10.3 a; ELD Part I, C, 10, 12 and ELD Part II, A-C)	Create a poem or personal narrative reflecting on a challenging relationship
Academic Writing Task (Aligns with CCSS.ELA-LITERACY.W.9-10.1; W.9-10.4-6; L.9-10.1 a, b; L.9-10.2 a-c; L.9-10.3 a; ELD Part I, C, 11, 12 and ELD Part II, A-C)	Analyze theme and its development in poem

INTRODUCTION

Holding a grudge is like letting someone live rent-free in our brain. The ability to soften our heart around someone who has let us down or harmed us in some more significant way and see them in the fullness of who they are beyond our small, uncomfortable duet, is mind- and heart-expanding. It's a brave act that benefits everyone, particularly ourselves.

In the poem "Revenge," the speaker searches high and low for an excuse not to take his revenge. He is working with his own hatred rather than being ruled by it. He understands that forgiveness is not just about the other person but also about fulfilling his own potential as a human being. Through his musings on all the people who love his enemy or have some positive association with him, he can loosen the grip of hatred on his own heart.

DID YOU KNOW? TRAINING OURSELVES TO FORGIVE

The inability to forgive is one of the main sources of stress in a person's life. Ruminating about negative experiences in the past and fantasizing about future revenge is a nonadaptive coping strategy detrimental to our well-being. Fortunately, researchers have found that many of the skills gained through mindfulness practice, such as nonreactivity, nonjudgment, and perspective-taking can help us to forgive. Through the practice of watching our thoughts and realizing their repetitive and damaging nature, we can free ourselves from their grip.

However, as world-renowned psychologist, author, and teacher Jack Kornfield notes, forgiveness isn't sentimental or quick. He describes it as a "deep process of the heart" that involves honoring all the emotions that the betrayal evoked—shock, disbelief, grief, anger, and fear. By allowing ourselves to fully tap into these emotions and experience them in our bodies, we gain insight into how holding on to resentment isn't being compassionate with ourselves. It doesn't mean that we condone what happened or necessitate that we be in contact with the person who has harmed us. In itself, setting an intention to no longer allow ourselves to be defined by our suffering is a powerful step in the direction of healing.

In the high-stress teaching profession, remaining emotionally balanced and being able to forgive social transgressions is critical. Research studies have shown that mindfulness training for teachers aimed at fortifying this prosocial skill has proven effective. Teachers were able to decide to forgive through seeing the larger picture and realizing that holding on to resentment was causing themselves harm.

STUDENT LESSON OBJECTIVES

- ✔ Call to mind a difficult interaction you recently had with someone and notice the emotions and sensations that come up for you
- ✔ Experiment with forgiveness practice
- ✔ Do a close reading of the poem "Revenge" by Taha Muhammad Ali and answer questions about it
- ✔ Write your own version of the poem or a story inspired by it
- ✔ Write a paragraph sharing what you think the poet's message is and prove it with lines from the poem

Step 1: Quick Write (5 min.) and Partner Share (5 min.)

Prompt: Write about a difficult interaction you had with someone during the past week.

Step 2: Guided Practice (5–7 min.)

Teacher Note: Forgiveness can be a sensitive topic for students. You might like to share Kornfield's understanding of forgiveness in the "Did You Know?" section before beginning this practice. Similar to compassion, forgiveness begins at home. Finding peace in our own hearts for the ways we judge or criticize ourselves prepares us to extend the wish for well-being to others.

Script

As we begin the practice of forgiveness, let's keep in mind our common humanity—the fact that, despite our differences, everyone wishes to be happy. So, check in to see how your body is feeling today—maybe twist your spine and circle your wrists and ankles, making sure everything is still working. (Pause.)

Now come to stillness and notice your feet on the floor, the support of the chair, and these few moments we have to be together and reconnect with ourselves in silence. (Pause and ring bell.) *Notice the rhythm of your breath entering and exiting your nostrils, the rise and fall of your belly and chest . . . like waves on the ocean, coming and going, coming and going, sustaining our lives.* (Pause.)

And maybe, just for today, we can set an intention to be kind to ourselves, to do no harm through our thoughts or words. (Pause.) *Recognize the many ways in which we belittle and punish ourselves through our internal dialogues. Practice being at peace with ourselves just as we are . . . without needing to change anything . . . just as we might observe a tree in the forest. No matter how straight or twisted, solid and healthy, or hollowed out and decayed, we can see its unique beauty and accept it as it is.* (Pause.) *Soften your heart and breathe in a feeling of acceptance and forgiveness.* (Pause.)

Now, call to mind someone with whom you've had a difficult interaction recently, maybe a parent or sibling who invaded your space or didn't respond to your needs in the way you would have liked . . . maybe a friend who excluded you from a party or said something hurtful. (Pause.)

Connect with any emotions that arise—sadness, hurt, anger, and any sensations in your body as you recall this memory, maybe a heaviness in your chest or a tightness in your belly—and allow it to be as it is. (Pause.) *If it feels comfortable, you might like to bring a hand to your heart or your belly, in a gesture of love and care for this pain and sorrow.* (Pause.)

Now imagine your friend or family member being happy, doing something they love. (Pause.) *See the joy on their face . . . being mindful of the fact that those who harm us do so because they themselves are suffering. See if you can connect with their pain and sorrow, their disappointments and grief.*

Now, if it feels appropriate, offer them forgiveness and wish them well-being and ease. "I forgive you. May you be happy and at ease." And if you're not ready at this time, say instead, "May I be able to forgive at some time in the future, and may I take care of my own heart as it continues to hold the weight of this sorrow." (Invite a student to ring the bell.)

Step 3: Debrief (partners, then whole class, 5–10 min.)

1. What did you notice?
2. Were you able to forgive yourself for something?
3. What other relationship came to mind? How did you imagine this person being happy?

Step 4: Watch Video: "Revenge" (6 min.)

Play video of poetry reading.

Step 5: Making Connections

1. How do you feel after watching this reading?
2. What do you appreciate about it?
3. What images do you remember?

Step 6: Cloze Listening Activity (Handout A) (10 min.)

Distribute the listening worksheet and, after reviewing unfamiliar vocabulary, read poem aloud and have students fill in the missing words.

Step 7: Text-Dependent Questions (Handout B; Answers on Handout C) (15–20 min.)

Distribute Handout B for students to complete questions, either alone, with a partner, or in small groups.

Step 8: Text Response (Handout B; Sample Response on Handout C)

Prompt: What's ironic about the poem title? Is the poem's theme actually about getting revenge? At what state of mind has the speaker arrived by the end of his meditation on forgiveness?

Step 9: Self-Reflection (Handout B)

Prompt: What character traits does forgiveness require? How might taking a wider view of a challenging person in your life, beyond your personal difficulties, free you from judgment and hate?

Step 10: Poem Writing (Handout D, E, or F) (10–15 min.)

Distribute Handout D, E, or F, depending on students' fluency in English and creative writing experience.

Step 11: Prose Writing Option

Prompt: Write a letter to someone who has hurt you. Imagine the other relationships in their life, and the fact that, just like you, they wish to be happy. See if you can find a way to unburden your own heart by letting go.

TAKEAWAY

The theme of forgiveness is rich terrain to explore with students. If they are willing to fully explore how this practice benefits them, not only will their hearts be lighter, but their minds will also be better able to focus on academics.

EXTENSION

For homework, invite students to undertake the following creative visualization exercise. Have them set the intention to release their pain and suffering and be free. You might suggest that they record the following script on their cell phones and replay it for themselves.

Script

Take your seat and drop into the body. Turn off your inner smartphone, the thinking mind, for a few moments and enjoy a few deep, relaxing breaths. When you are ready, imagine someone with whom you've had difficulty sitting in front of you, open to hearing what you have to say. Let them know why you are angry with them and how they've hurt you. Express all the hurt, the disappointment, the dashed expectations, hopes, and dreams. Then, when you feel you have nothing left that is burdening your heart, become quiet and notice what arises in the stillness. You may become aware that the person you're imagining sitting before you is also hurting in some way and in need of an apology.

Revenge
by Taha Muhammad Ali

At times . . . I wish
I could meet in a duel
the man who killed my father
and razed our home,
5 expelling me
into
a narrow country.
And if he killed me,
I'd rest at last,
10 and if I were ready—
I would take my revenge!

*

But if it came to light,
when my rival appeared,
that he had a mother
15 waiting for him,
or a father who'd put

his right hand over
the heart's place in his chest
whenever his son was late
20 even by just a quarter-hour
for a meeting they'd set—
then I would not kill him,
even if I could.

*

Likewise . . . I
25 would not murder him
if it were soon made clear
that he had a brother or sisters
who loved him and constantly longed to see him.
Or if he had a wife to greet him
30 and children who
couldn't bear his absence
and whom his gifts would thrill.
Or if he had
friends or companions,
35 neighbors he knew
or allies from prison
or a hospital room,
or classmates from his school . . .
asking about him
40 and sending him regards.

*

But if he turned
out to be on his own—
cut off like a branch from a tree—
without a mother or father,
45 with neither a brother nor sister,
wifeless, without a child,
and without kin or neighbors or friends,
colleagues or companions,
then I'd add not a thing to his pain
50 within that aloneness—
not the torment of death,
and not the sorrow of passing away.
Instead I'd be content
to ignore him when I passed him by

55 on the street—as I
convinced myself
that paying him no attention
in itself was a kind of revenge.

Handout A

Cloze Listening Activity

Name: ______________________________

Listen to the poem and use the words to fill in the blanks.

regards	allies	branch	wifeless	colleagues	torment	kin
razed	duel	rival	quarter-hour	longed	rest	ignore
expelling	narrow	clear	revenge	bear	convinced	

Revenge
by Taha Muhammad Ali

At times . . . I wish
I could meet in a (1) ____________________
the man who killed my father
and (2) ____________________ our home,
5 (3) ____________________ me
into
a (4) ____________________ country.
And if he killed me,
I'd (5) ____________________ at last,
10 and if I were ready—
I would take my revenge!

*

But if it came to light,
when my (6) ____________________ appeared,
that he had a mother
15 waiting for him,
or a father who'd put
his right hand over
the heart's place in his chest
whenever his son was late

Continued on next page

20 even by just a (7) __________________
for a meeting they'd set—
then I would not kill him,
even if I could.

*

Likewise . . . I
25 would not murder him
if it were soon made (8) __________________
that he had a brother or sisters
who loved him and constantly (9) __________________ to see him.
Or if he had a wife to greet him
30 and children who
couldn't (10) __________________ his absence
and whom his gifts would thrill.
Or if he had
friends or companions,
35 neighbors he knew
or (11) __________________ from prison
or a hospital room,
or classmates from his school . . .
asking about him
40 and sending him (12) __________________.

*

But if he turned
out to be on his own—
cut off like a (13) __________________ from a tree—
without a mother or father,
45 with neither a brother nor sister,
(14) __________________, without a child,
and without (15) __________________ or neighbors or friends,

Continued on next page

(16) _________________ or companions,
then I'd add not a thing to his pain
50 within that aloneness—
not the (17) _________________ of death,
and not the sorrow of passing away.
Instead I'd be content
to (18) _________________ him when I passed him by
55 on the street—as I
(19) _________________ myself
that paying him no attention
in itself was a kind of (20) _________________.

Handout B

Text-Dependent Questions, Text Response, and Personal Reflection

Name: ____________________________

Text-Dependent Questions

1. What does the word "duel" mean in line 2? Use context clues.

____

____

2. In line 8, the speaker says, "And if he killed me,/I'd rest at last." Why can't he rest?

____

____

3. How does the use of the conditional (i.e., "At times I wish I could") show the poet's attitude toward his subject (tone) and his message (theme)? Find one more line that illustrates this.

____

____

4. In line 14, the speaker imagines a mother waiting for his rival. List eight other relationships he mentions that his enemy has.

____

____

5. A shift happens in the speaker's thinking beginning in line 12: "But if it came to light." Describe how he changes his perspective.

____

____

6. Where else in the poem do we notice a shift in the speaker's thinking and feeling about his enemy? How does this change heighten his empathy, or at least lessen his desire to seek revenge?

____

____

Continued on next page

Text Response

Examine the theme and its development in the poem.

Prompt

What's ironic about the poem title? Is the poem's theme actually about getting revenge? What state of mind has the speaker arrived at by the end of his meditation on forgiveness? Find lines from the poem (cite textual evidence) to show your understanding.

____

____

____

____

Self-Reflection

What character traits does forgiveness require? How might taking a wider view of a challenging person in your life, beyond your personal difficulties, free you from judgment and hate?

____

____

____

____

Handout C

Text-Dependent Questions Answer Key and Sample Text Response

Text-Dependent Questions Answer Key

1. A duel is a deadly contest between two people to settle a question of honor.
2. because he is being tormented by his hatred
3. The tone is uncertain and the speaker in Ali's poem is not convinced that taking revenge is the right course of action; "if he killed me"; "if I were ready"
4. father, brother, sisters, children, friends, companions, neighbors, allies, classmates
5. He no longer wishes his enemy harm as he imagines other people who have positive feelings toward him.
6. In line 41—"but if he turned/out to be on his own"—the speaker seems to be taking to heart how lonely and isolated his enemy would be without people in his life who cared about him; he empathizes with him.

Sample Text Response

The poem's title, "Revenge," is ironic because the poem is actually a meditation on empathy and finding a path to forgiveness. By imagining the loving relationships in his enemy's life, the speaker is able to gain a broader perspective on him and begin to soften his hatred. In lines 24–28, he says, "I/would not murder him/if it were soon made clear/ that he had a brother or sisters/who loved him and constantly longed to see him."

Toward the end of the poem, the speaker shifts toward imagining his rival alone in the world, and here his empathy becomes clear, even as it is still tinged with some vengeful feelings—"then I'd add not a thing to his pain/within that aloneness—not the torment of death,/and not the sorrow of passing away." While he's not fully ready to forgive his enemy, he also doesn't wish him harm. The speaker ends by convincing himself that ignoring him if they passed each other on the street would be "a kind of revenge," which illustrates how difficult the journey to completely forgive someone is.

Handout D

Basic Poem Writing Play Sheet

Name: ______________________________

Copy your favorite line from the poem below:

____

Next, brainstorm three to five words in the categories below:

Ways to Hurt Someone (action verbs)	Relatives

Now fill in the blanks with your own ideas from the chart.

At times I wish I could ________________ ________________
(action verb) *("enemy")*

but I know their ________________ loves them,
(relative)

so I wouldn't hurt them even if I could.

Continued on next page

Draw a picture of your “enemy” being happy.

Handout E

Intermediate Poem Writing Play Sheet

Name: ______________________________

Brainstorm words in the following categories, and then use your ideas to write your own version of the poem.

Ways to physically harm someone	Relatives	Ways to show concern

Continued on next page

Title: ____

(save the title for last and make it surprising or just right for your words)

At times I wish

I could ____
(How might you imagine harming someone who has hurt you?)

______________________ who ____
(enemy) *(concrete example of how s/he has caused harm)*

and ____.
(concrete example of how s/he has caused harm)

But if it came to light,

when __________________________ appeared,
(enemy)

that __________ had a ________________ who _____________________________
(pron.) *(relative)* *(How do they show their concern?)*

and a ________________ who _______________________________
(relative) *(How do they show their concern?)*

then I would not harm __________,
(pron.)

even if I could.

Handout F

Advanced Poem Writing Play Sheet

Name: ______________________________

Use the following template as a guide to write your own version of the poem. Feel free to change it or abandon it at any point.

Title: ____
(save the title for last and make it surprising or just right for your words)

At times I wish

I could ____

who ____

But if it came to light,

when ____________________ appeared,

that ____________ had a ____________________ who ____________________________

and a ____________________ who ____________________________

then I would not harm ____________________, even if I could.

CREATIVE WRITING EXAMPLES

Poetry

At times I wish
I could meet in a duel
the girl who spilled water on my tablet
and scattered rumors about me at school.

But if it came to light,
when the girl appeared,
that she had a little brother who cried
when she left for school in the morning
and jumped up and down when she returned at night
and a mother who texted her "I love you" every day at noon,
then I would not harm her,
even if I could.

—Demi, seventh grade

At times I wish
I could skin him alive while he watches,
the man who made me unlovable
And unintentionally preoccupied his life with everything but me.

But if it came to light,
when the man appeared,
that he had a niece who loved to Facetime,
and a mother who depended on him,
then I would not harm him,
even if I could.

—Sammi, eleventh grade

Prose

A Letter of Forgiveness

I want to forgive you for hurting me. I know now that it's because you were hurting. As the saying goes, "Hurt people hurt other people." You needed space and time, and I didn't give you that. We both need to forgive ourselves and each other. I do wish you had communicated with me because I just assumed you hated me, and it caused me a lot of anxiety. I couldn't eat, sleep, or concentrate on school or anything else. I still care about you, just in a different way. I hope you feel the same.

—Teddy Bear, ninth grade

Release

No matter how hard this is, I know that people love you and want you to be happy—your friends, your mother, your sisters. Perhaps you've met someone new with whom you've been able to unburden your heart. I hope so. I want you to be happy, and the tightness in my breast to soften, to acknowledge that I loved you and then experience the momentary thrill of throwing rose petals from a high bridge and watching them flutter and fall and marveling at the beauty of their passing away, their slipping from my hands.

—Laura Bean (author)

REFERENCES, RESOURCES, AND FURTHER READING

Ali, Taha Muhammad. "Revenge." Geraldine R. Dodge Poetry Festival. Video of poetry reading, 6:44. Uploaded September 18, 2006. www.youtube.com/watch?v=K4fpjDUl1vk (accessed August 1, 2022).

Braun, Summer S., S. Cho, B. A. Colaianne, C. Taylor, M. Cullen, and R. W. Roeser. "Impacts of a Mindfulness-Based Program on Teachers' Forgiveness." *Mindfulness* 11, no. 8 (August 2020): 1978–92.

de la Fuente-Anuncibay, R., Á. González-Barbadillo, D. Ortega-Sánchez, N. Ordóñez-Camblor, and J. P. Pizarro-Ruiz. "Anger Rumination and Mindfulness: Mediating Effects on Forgiveness." *International Journal of Environmental Research and Public Health* 18, no. 5 (March 2021): 2668.

Kornfield, Jack. "The Ancient Art of Forgiveness." August 23, 2011. https://greatergood.berkeley.edu/article/item/the_ancient_heart_of_forgiveness (accessed August 1, 2022).

Lesson Twelve

Joy

"Everything Is Waiting for You" by David Whyte

"Yes, I am imperfect and vulnerable and sometimes afraid, but that doesn't change the truth that I am also brave and worthy of love and belonging."

~ Brené Brown

OBJECTIVES

Mindfulness Skill	Explore open awareness practice
CASEL Framework Highlights	Self-awareness: link feelings, values, and thoughts Self-management: manage one's emotions; identify and use stress-management techniques
Creative Writing Task (Aligns with CCSS.ELA-LITERACY.W.9-10.3 a-e; W.9-10.4-6; L.9-10.1 a,b; L.9-10.2 a-c; L.9-10.3 a; ELD Part I, C, 10, 12 and ELD Part II, A-C)	Write a poem or letter of appreciation celebrating our interconnectedness with all that surrounds us
Academic Writing Task (Aligns with CCSS.ELA-LITERACY.W.9-10.1; W.9-10.4-6; L.9-10.1 a, b; L.9-10.2 a-c; L.9-10.3 a; ELD Part I, C, 11, 12 and ELD Part II, A-C)	Analyze theme and its development over course of poem

INTRODUCTION

We are all players in the game of life. We can choose how we want to orient ourselves—as isolated victims or as spiritual beings connected to everything and everyone. Mindfulness allows us to see the bigger picture of who we are. We're bigger than the stories of inadequacy and isolation we create out of fear (or the parallel stories of aggrandizement we create to mask our insecurities). By becoming intimate with the workings of our own minds and questioning our personal narratives, we may arrive at a felt sense of the interconnectedness of self and others. This can give our lives greater meaning and purpose. We are not alone.

DID YOU KNOW? HUMAN FLOURISHING: CULTIVATING HEALTHY HABITS OF MIND

Researchers have identified four core dimensions of well-being—awareness, connection, insight, and purpose. Each of these areas can be viewed as skills that can be learned through practice. Because of neuroplasticity, this intentional training can actually change our brains. There's even an app for us to chart our progress. Richard Davidson, professor of psychology and psychiatry at the University of Wisconsin–Madison and founder and chair of the Center for Healthy Minds, and his team developed the Healthy Minds app to provide individuals with accessible micro interventions and the ability to assess their own growth in each of the four areas. Let's break each of these four areas down:

Awareness

Awareness (mindfulness) of our perceptions of what's going on around us as well as inside of us helps us develop greater focus and calm. We know where our mind is and what it's doing. From this embodied presence, we are able to recognize when we're distracted by a thought, triggered by an emotion, or simply on autopilot, and we are able to curb our impulses and redirect our attention back to our current activity, whether it is driving a car, having a conversation with someone, or taking an exam. Awareness plays a pivotal role in regulating our emotions, which is vital to our physical and mental health, and in controlling our behavior to achieve our goals.

Connection

We are social beings. Connection allows us to bring a more spacious and loving orientation toward ourselves and those around us. Appreciating the positive qualities and beneficial actions of others helps us to perceive the world as a friendlier place. Recalling our common humanity allows us to extend ourselves to those perceived to be different. People who demonstrate empathy and have altruistic aims experience higher levels of well-being.

Insight

Insight refers to gaining greater perspective on how our thoughts, feelings, and beliefs shape our sense of self. When we gain self-knowledge and get curious about our self-narrative, we can turn the mind into an ally. For example, when we feel anxious, we're able to step back in the moment and see how self-critical thoughts or memories may be tainting our perception of reality and creating fearful expectations. We can then recalibrate and direct our minds in a more wholesome direction. Developing insight is pivotal to contemporary psychiatry and psychotherapy, and it has been linked to a number of healthy attributes, such as the ability to perceive social cues and regulate emotions.

Purpose

Purpose involves clarity about our aims and values; it's what gives our lives meaning and allows us to direct our behavior in life-affirming ways. A strong sense of purpose has also been linked to more positive health outcomes, such as increased physical activity and a reduction in stress and emotional reactivity.

However, it's interesting to note that all values are not created equal when it comes to well-being. Grounding ourselves in intrinsic values and goals, particularly those related to the greater good, positively influence our well-being. In contrast, pursuing extrinsic, materialistic goals diminish it.

STUDENT LESSON OBJECTIVES

- ✔ Practice mindfulness in a relaxed way with your eyes open
- ✔ Do a close reading of the poem "Everything Is Waiting for You" by David Whyte and answer questions about it
- ✔ Write your own version of the poem or a story inspired by it
- ✔ Write a paragraph sharing what you think the poet's message is and prove it with lines from the poem

Step 1: Quick Write (5 min.) and Partner Share (5 min.)

Prompt: List ten things you use every day that help you, even in some small way.

Step 2: Guided Open Awareness Practice (5–7 min.)

Teacher Note: If possible, lead this practice outside in a relatively quiet place, free from distraction. Ideally, students could practice lying down on blankets in the grass. If you're unable to go outside, adjust the script as needed, remembering that grounding one's attention in the five senses can happen anywhere.

Script

(Ring bell.) *Now get comfortable on your blanket or mat, feeling the ground beneath you, this welcoming bed for your head, shoulders, back, hips, legs, and feet. Allow yourself to sink into your body resting on the earth—feel the weight of your skull, your eyes softening more deeply in their sockets. Close your eyes if you wish and drop into your heart.* (Pause.) *Allow a half-smile to form around your eyes and mouth. Feel a spontaneous joy arise for no reason.* (Pause.)

Find the breath in your body, perhaps the sensation of the air in your nostrils or the rise and fall of your belly and chest. And for the next few breaths, bring your full attention to your inhalation . . . and your exhalation. (Pause.)

If thoughts of What's for lunch? *or* Did I remember my homework? *arise, just gently label them "thinking" and return to your breath.* (Pause.) *See your thoughts pass through your mind like clouds in the sky. Accept all of them and their attendant emotions—joy and sorrow, confusion and clarity, fear and anxiety, contentment and ease. Things are what they are, and no thought or emotion is permanent.* (Pause.)

Enjoy this sense of stability in your mind, and now let go of all your efforts. Just relax without doing anything or trying to make anything happen. Leave your mind alone. If you've closed your eyes, you might like to open them, taking in the shapes and colors of objects around you. . . . (Pause.) *Feel a sense of kinship with the natural world and appreciate this moment of belonging.* (Pause for a few moments or minutes, depending on the audience; then invite a student to ring the bell.)

Step 3: Debrief (partners, then whole class, 5–10 min.)

1. How did it feel to practice outside? *(if appropriate)*
2. Did you experiment with keeping with your eyes open?
3. What colors and shapes did you notice?
4. Were you aware of any thoughts that arose? Did you label the thoughts "thinking"? Did any emotions follow the thoughts? Which ones?

Step 4: Read "Everything Is Waiting for You" (2 min.)

Read poem aloud. Encourage students to visualize what they hear.

Step 5: Making Connections (5–10 min.)

1. What do you appreciate about the poem?
2. What words or phrases or images do you remember?
3. How do you feel after hearing it?

Step 6: Cloze Listening Activity (Handout A) (10 min.)

Review unfamiliar vocabulary and do a part-of-speech sort. Then read the poem aloud a second time or have a volunteer do so, pausing while students fill in the missing words.

Step 7: Text-Dependent Questions (Handout B; Answers on Handout C) (15–20 min.)

Distribute Handout B for students to complete questions, either alone, with a partner, or in small groups.

Step 8: Text Response

Prompt: Why does Whyte say that "everything is waiting for you"? What phrases does he use to convince us of this?

Step 9: Self-Reflection

Prompt: How can becoming more self-aware help you connect more easily to others? Give an example from your life.

Step 10: Poem Writing (Handout D, E, or F) (10–15 min.)

Distribute Handout D, E, or F, depending on students' fluency in English and creative writing experience.

Step 11: Prose Writing Option

Prompt: Write a letter of appreciation to the things that surround you.

TAKEAWAY

Training our awareness in acceptance and self-compassion allows us to face whatever arises in consciousness with equanimity. The grip of negative storylines about self and other loosens, and we experience greater freedom and joy.

EXTENSION

Write a letter of gratitude to someone who has supported you this year. Mention a specific example of a time when they showed up for you and what you learned from them.

Everything Is Waiting for You
by David Whyte

Your great mistake is to act the drama
as if you were alone. As if life
were a progressive and cunning crime
with no witness to the tiny hidden
5 transgressions. To feel abandoned is to deny
the intimacy of your surroundings. Surely,
even you, at times, have felt the grand array;
the swelling presence, and the chorus, crowding
out your solo voice. You must note
10 the way the soap dish enables you,
or the window latch grants you freedom.
Alertness is the hidden discipline of familiarity.
The stairs are your mentor of things
to come, the doors have always been there
15 to frighten you and invite you,
and the tiny speaker in the phone
is your dream-ladder to divinity.

Put down the weight of your aloneness and ease into
the conversation. The kettle is singing
20 even as it pours you a drink, the cooking pots
have left their arrogant aloofness and
seen the good in you at last. All the birds
and creatures of the world are unutterably
themselves. Everything is waiting for you.

Handout A

Cloze Listening Activity

Name: ______________________________

Directions: Sort the words below by parts of speech. Remember that nouns may be abstract (conceptual) as well as concrete.

alertness	aloneness	array	arrogant	crowding out
cunning	deny	drama	dream-ladder	ease into
enables	familiarity	grants	intimacy	mentor
progressive	swelling	transgressions	waiting	witness

Glossary

array (n.)—an impressive display of something

note (v.)—recognize, see, understand

enables (v.)—helps, supports

grants (v.)—gives, offers

swelling (adj.)—becoming greater

Adjective	Noun	Verb
progressive	alertness—the state of being alert	ease into

Continued on next page

Now fill in the blanks with the missing words below.

Everything Is Waiting for You
by David Whyte

Your great mistake is to act the (1) ________________
as if you were alone. As if life
were a (2) ________________ and (3) ________________ crime
with no (4) ________________ to the tiny hidden
5 (5) ________________. To feel abandoned is to (6) ________________
the (7) ________________ of your surroundings. Surely,
even you, at times, have felt the grand (8) ________________;
the (9) ________________ presence, and the chorus, (10) ________________
________________ your solo voice. You must note
10 the way the soap dish (11) ________________ you,
or the window latch (12) ________________ you freedom.
(13) ________________ is the hidden discipline of (14) ________________.
The stairs are your (15) ________________ of things
to come, the doors have always been there
15 to frighten you and invite you,
and the tiny speaker in the phone
is your (16) ________________ to divinity.

Put down the weight of your (17) ________________ and (18) ________________
the conversation. The kettle is singing
20 even as it pours you a drink, the cooking pots
have left their (19) ________________ aloofness and
seen the good in you at last. All the birds
and creatures of the world are unutterably
themselves. Everything is (20) ________________ for you.

Handout B

Text-Dependent Questions, Text Response, and Personal Reflection

Name: ______________________________

Text-Dependent Questions

1. Nominalization is the use of a verb or an adjective as an abstract noun. For example, in line 12—"Alertness is the hidden discipline of familiarity"—*alertness* comes from the adjective "alert" and *familiarity* comes from the adjective "familiar." Find one more example.

____

____

2. The poem begins with these words: "Your great mistake is to act the drama/as if you were alone" (1–2). How does the person who is addressed in the poem feel?

____

____

3. What does the word "transgression" mean in the line, "with no witness to the tiny hidden transgressions" (4–5)? Use context clues.

____

____

4. In lines 9–10, the poet says, "You must note/the way the soap dish enables you." This is an example of personification, giving human qualities to something nonhuman. Find two more examples.

____

____

5. In line 12, the speaker says, "Alertness is the hidden discipline of familiarity." Why is the poet emphasizing the importance of staying awake when we are in familiar surroundings? What can you guess (infer) from this line?

____

____

6. What is Whyte's attitude toward us, the reader (tone)? What lines or phrases show it?

____

____

Continued on next page

Text Response

Examine the theme and its development in the poem.

Prompt

Why does Whyte say that "everything is waiting for you"? What phrases does he use to convince us? Cite textual evidence.

____

____

____

____

____

____

Self-Reflection

How can becoming more self-aware help you connect more easily to others? Give an example from your life.

____

____

____

____

____

____

Handout C

Text-Dependent Questions Answer Key and Sample Text Response

Text-Dependent Questions Answer Key

1. intimacy, aloneness, aloofness
2. alone, abandoned
3. a crime or offense; "to feel abandoned"; "the grand array"
4. "the window latch grants you freedom"; "the doors . . . frighten you and invite you"; "the kettle . . . pours you a drink"; "the cooking pots have left their arrogant aloofness and seen the good in you at last"
5. We can get lazy with our own minds and around those we most love. We must practice being aware of our thoughts and feelings, so we don't fall into unhealthy habits of mind. It's important to continuously offer compassion to ourselves and our loved ones.
6. Encouraging, persuasive; "Surely even you, at times, have felt the grand array"; "Put down the weight of your aloneness and ease into the conversation."

Sample Text Response

Whyte titled this poem "Everything Is Waiting for You" to remind us that feeling connected is a choice. In lines 6–9, he chides us to move beyond our old storylines: "Surely,/even you, at times, have felt the grand array;/the swelling presence, and the chorus, crowding/ out your solo voice." We must practice discipline and self-reflection to see the bigger picture of who we are and how we are related to everyone and everything. By challenging our negative self-talk and storylines, particularly in community with others, we gain the insight that our suffering is not unique. By offering ourselves compassion, we become more available to support those around us in need.

Handout D

Basic Poem Writing Play Sheet

Name: ______________________________

Copy your favorite line from the poem "Everything Is Waiting for You."

____

Next, brainstorm three to five words in each category below:

Kinds of Entertainment	Everyday Objects

Glossary

note (v.)—recognize, see, understand

enables (v.)—helps, supports

grants (v.)—gives, offers

Continued on next page

Now, use your ideas to fill in the blanks below:

Your great mistake is to act the ________________________________
(kind of entertainment)
as if you were alone.

You must note the way the ________________________________ enables you
(everyday object)
or the ________________________________ grants you freedom.
(everyday object)

Draw a picture of your most joyful, connected self.

Handout E

Intermediate Poem Writing Play Sheet

Name: ______________________________

Brainstorm words in the following categories, and then use your ideas to write your own version of the poem.

Challenges/ difficulties	Experiences of connection	Household objects	What this object could do for you	Things from nature

Continued on next page

HANDOUT E 2 / 2

Title: ____
(save the title for last and make it surprising or just right for your words)

Your great mistake is to act the drama

as if you were alone. As if life

were ____
(challenge/difficulty)

To feel abandoned is to deny

the intimacy of your surroundings. Surely,

even you, at times, have felt ____
(an experience that gives you a positive feeling of connection)

You must note the way the ______________________________ enables you
(everyday object)

or the ______________________________ grants you freedom.
(everyday object)

Put down the weight of your aloneness and ease into the

conversation. The ______________________________ is singing
(household object that makes sound)

even as it ____________________________________
(something this object does for you)

All the ____ are unutterably
(something from nature)

themselves. Everything is waiting for you.

Handout F

Advanced Poem Writing Play Sheet

Name: ______________________________

Use the following template as a guide to write your own version of the poem. Feel free to change it or abandon it at any point.

Title: ____

(save the title for last and make it surprising or just right for your words)

Your great mistake is to act the drama

as if you were alone. As if life

were ____

To feel abandoned is to deny

the intimacy of your surroundings. Surely,

even you, at times, have felt ____

You must note the way the ____ enables you

or the ____ grants you freedom.

Put down the weight of your aloneness and ease into the

conversation. The ____ is singing

even as it ____

All the ____ are unutterably

themselves. Everything is waiting for you.

HANDOUT F

CREATIVE WRITING EXAMPLES

Poetry

Beach Day

Your great mistake is to act the drama
as if you were alone. As if life
were a waking up on a cold morning.
To feel abandoned is to deny
the intimacy of your surroundings. Surely,
even you, at times, have felt the joy of laughing with friends.
You must note the way the sand enables you
or the ocean grants you freedom.
Put down the weight of your aloneness and ease
into the conversation. The radio is singing
even as it starts to crackle.
All the trees are unutterably
themselves. Everything is waiting for you.

—David, eleventh grade

Affection

Your great mistake is to act the drama
as if you were alone. As if life
were a disheartening string of emails
from someone you once dearly loved.
To feel abandoned is to deny
the intimacy of your surroundings. Surely,
even you, at times, have felt your cat's eyes
gaze into yours with true affection.
You must note the way the paper clip enables you
or the doorknob grants you freedom.
Put down the weight of your aloneness and ease
into the conversation. The air purifier is singing
even as it drowns out the street noise.
All the turkeys who parade down Jackson Street are unutterably
themselves. Everything is waiting for you.

—Laura Bean (author)

Prose

To my friend, the garden,

You are my silent partner in all the machinations of my mind. Thank you for reminding me to be quiet and rest, that all things are not within my control and that there's a season for everything and everyone, and that, alas, nothing lasts. The lemon tree is pint-size, like me, and it's healthy and bearing fruit. Thanks for the lemons and the reminder to be courageous. To the princess bush, who I first met when I moved to California. Thank you for letting me know that trees can blossom purple and reminding me how regal I am no matter my address. In my garden, everything belongs, surrounding me with health, vitality, and potentiality. I belong here in the nature of things.

—Laura Bean (author)

REFERENCES, RESOURCES, AND FURTHER READING

Dahl, Cortland J., Christine D. Wilson-Mendenhall, and Richard J. Davidson. "The Plasticity of Well-Being: A Training-Based Framework for the Cultivation of Human Flourishing." *Proceedings of the National Academy of Sciences* 117, no. 51 (December 2020): 32197–206.

Davidson, Richard. "How Mindfulness Changes the Emotional Life of our Brains. TEDx San Francisco. Video of lecture, 17:53. Uploaded October 3, 2019. www.ted.com/talks /richard_j_davidson_how_mindfulness_changes_the_emotional_life_of_our_brains _jan_2019?language=en (accessed August 1, 2022).

———. "Mindfulness and More: Toward a Science of Human Flourishing." *Psychosomatic Medicine* 83, no. 6 (July–August 2021): 665–68.

Whyte, David. "David Whyte on Poetry and Poem 'Everything Is Waiting for You.'" Interview on New Dimensions Radio. Recorded December 1, 2007. Video montage and recording of interview, 3:28. www.youtube.com/watch?v=hq2NfrNt9EU (accessed August 1, 2022).

Culminating Activities

“Take time to celebrate the quiet miracles that seek no attention.”

~ John O’Donohue

OBJECTIVES

Mindfulness Skill	Bring awareness to bear in daily interactions and performance tasks
CASEL Competencies Highlights	Social awareness: recognize strengths in others, show concern for others’ feelings Relationship skills: practice teamwork and collaborative problem-solving, show leadership in groups
Creative Writing Task	Create a portfolio of favorite writing
Academic Writing Task Academic Speaking Tasks	Develop and strengthen writing by revising, editing, and proofreading Engage in collaborative discussions with peers and teacher Practice public speaking skills

INTRODUCTION

Students write best when there's an authentic audience for their work, whether it be their peers, their families, or the larger community. The writing they produce in an environment steeped in mindfulness is intimate and impactful. Sharing it with others facing the same challenges moving into adulthood, with its attendant doubts and fears, reinforces our common humanity and boosts empathy and compassion. It's also a cause for celebration—students often express pride and amazement at becoming published authors.

PUBLICATION

If you choose to create an anthology as a culminating activity, it's helpful to set the tone by having a planning meeting in which everyone has a voice and accepts responsibility for the end goal. Ask for volunteers to serve as editors, illustrators, and providers of tech support. Next, create a timeline leading up to publication, determining when the first draft will be compiled and all illustrations will be completed.

Ideally, students will have a wide selection of writing from which to choose. If they have submitted writing assignments on Google Classroom or another digital platform throughout the year, it will be relatively easy for them to review their work and create a final portfolio of three to five favorite poems or stories. From this, they can select which pieces they wish to include in the anthology. Everyone should be expected to contribute, and the editors can advise their hesitant peers on which pieces to include and lead them in revising, editing, and proofreading.

During the revision process, establish a safe environment in which students' work will be treated with interest and respect. It's important to stress the "process" element of writing. Let students know that even (and most especially) published authors work through multiple drafts of a piece. Like a sculptor working in clay, writers need to shape and mold their work. It's a creative endeavor that takes patience and persistence for one's best writing to emerge. Encourage them to add sensual details to create a vivid image in the reader's mind and to clarify any confusion. Reviewing the who, what, when, where, and why of their stories prompts them to fill in the details. Asking "what kind?" works wonders to move toward greater specificity.

One of my colleagues used the term "paperless" to refer to students who simply didn't write. The following story was written by one such student, a seventh-grade English Language Learner.

The Tennis Match

> My happy memory was when I played tennis with my friends in a park in Richmond last summer. We played doubles, with two friends on each team. It was a close game. The losers had to buy chips and juice for the winners. Our team won and enjoyed our victory. (Enrique, seventh grade, English learner)

Using his happy memory of playing tennis with his friends as a model for the class, I prompted him with questions about where they played and what the reward for the victors would be. My genuine interest and enthusiasm drew him into the community in a way that hadn't happened beforehand. It also helped his peers realize: (1) anyone can write, (2) the revision process can be fun, and (3) asking the writer extra questions to tease out details definitely improves a piece of writing.

As a draft gets closer to publication and line editing takes center stage, focus on strengthening verbs, choosing precise words for meaning and musicality, and being concise. Doing so will create clarity and bolster the author's voice. An enticing title and a surprising hook, two crucial elements to invite the reader in, are often best left for last.

Having all contributors brainstorm titles for the anthology helps to create buy-in and allows them to see the project as a whole. Ask illustrators to generate ideas for the cover design and support classmates in need of an illustration to accompany their pieces. These drawings should be simple black-and-white pencil drawings, traced with a black magic marker.

Upon publication, provide all students with a copy of the anthology and celebrate their accomplishments with a public reading and/or publishing party.

PUBLIC READING/PERFORMANCE

Mindfulness practice begins with embodiment—connecting with one's seat, one's breath, and one's senses. This awareness is also key to creating a dynamic, engaging reading. And because giving a presentation is a well-known stressor in both academic life and the work world, it's a wonderful opportunity for students to notice thoughts, feelings, and bodily sensations and any self-judgments that arise, then to offer themselves self-compassion.

For rehearsals, get students out of their desks. Have them practice walking at different speeds around the classroom and notice the effects on their body sensations and emotions. They can also take their writing in hand and, when signaled to stop, turn to a partner and take turns reading their work out loud. Whenever possible, have students rehearse outside, standing ten feet away from their partners to encourage projection, use of gesture, and eye contact.

Practicing reading to a tree or a bathroom mirror also helps students to become intimate with their writing and develop confidence in their voice. Encourage them to play with pregnant pauses and "punching" important words in each line to animate their writing.

To work on vocal projection, focus on abdominal breathing and forcefully making the sound "Ha! Ha! Ha!" while exhaling. This will help them connect with the power of their second "brain," the belly.

In the actual reading, give students the option of not only reading their own work, but also reading that of their peers. This is a beautiful form of recognition that students happily give each other.

Appendix

Curriculum Overview

Curriculum	Writing Theme	Mindfulness Practice	Self-awareness	Self-management	Social Awareness	Relationship Skills	Responsible Decision-making	Science/ Psychology
Lesson 1 Creating community	"Give a Little Love": positivity	yoga, 3 community breaths	X	X	X	X	X	Social engagement system
Lesson 2 The Gift of Attention	"The Summer Day": capturing a moment in detail	Listening to bell; 5 senses grounding ex.	X	X			X	Window of tolerance
Lesson 3 Belonging to natural world	"Song of Myself": Celebrating "larger" self	safe space creative visualization	X	X			X	Naturalist intelligence
Lesson 4 Why practice?	"Keeping Quiet": Benefits of stopping	counting breaths	X	X			X	Curiosity + academic success
Lesson 5 Self-compassion	"Kindness": Grief/loss	self-compassion break	X	X			X	Science of self-compassion
Lesson 6 Difficult emotions	"The Guest House": conflict	loving-kindness	X	X	X	X	X	Suffering = pain x resistance
Lesson 7 Acceptance	"So Much Happiness": gratitude	gratitude	X	X	X	X	X	Self-directed neuroplasticity
Lesson 8 Befriending oneself	"Love After Love": self-love	working with self-judgments	X	X			X	Self-talk
Lesson 9 Noticing habits	"Autobio. in 5 Short Chapters": patterns	habitual tendencies	X	X			X	Rewiring reward-based learning
Lesson 10 Empathy and compassion	"Saint Francis and the Sow": caring concern	compassion	X	X	X	X	X	Emotional resonance
Lesson 11 Forgiveness	"Revenge": challenging relationships	forgiveness	X	X	X	X	X	Forgiveness and healing
Lesson 12 Joy	"Everything Is Waiting for You": appreciation	open awareness	X	X			X	Healthy habits of mind

Lesson Routines	CCSS and ELD Standards Alignment
Step 1: Quick Write	ELD Part I: Interacting in Meaningful Ways C. Productive 10. Writing literary and informational texts to present, describe, and explain ideas and information, using appropriate technology, 12. Selecting and applying varied and precise vocabulary and other language resources to effectively convey ideas
GUIDED MINDFULNESS PRACTICE	
Step 2: Guided mindfulness	ELD Part I B. Interpretive 5. Listening actively to spoken English in a range of social and academic contexts
Step 3: Debrief	ELD Part I A. Collaborative 1. Exchanging information and ideas with others through oral collaborative discussions on a range of social and academic topics
READING AND DISCUSSION	
Step 4: Teacher reads poem	ELD Part I, B. 5.
Step 5: Making connections	ELD Part I, A. 1.
Step 6: Cloze listening	ELD Part I, B. 5 ELD Part I, B.6 Reading closely literary and informational texts and viewing multimedia to determine how meaning is conveyed explicitly and implicitly through language
Step 7: Text-dependent questions	CCSS.ELA-LITERACY.RL.9-10.1 Cite strong and thorough textual evidence to support analysis of what the text says explicitly as well as inferences drawn from the text. CCSS.ELA-LITERACY.RL.9-10.4 Determine the meaning of words and phrases as they are used in the text, including figurative and connotative meanings; analyze the cumulative impact of specific word choices on meaning and tone (e.g., how the language evokes a sense of time and place; how it sets a formal or informal tone). CCSS.ELA-LITERACY.L.9-10.4 Determine or clarify the meaning of unknown and multiple-meaning words and phrases based on *grades 9-10 reading and content*, choosing flexibly from a range of strategies. CCSS.ELA-LITERACY.L.9-10.4.A Use context (e.g., the overall meaning of a sentence, paragraph, or text; a word's position or function in a sentence) as a clue to the meaning of a word or phrase. CCSS.ELA-LITERACY.L.9-10.4.B Identify and correctly use patterns of word changes that indicate different meanings or parts of speech (e.g., *analyze, analysis, analytical; advocate, advocacy*). CCSS.ELA-LITERACY.L.9-10.4.C Consult general and specialized reference materials (e.g., dictionaries, glossaries, thesauruses), both print and digital, to find the pronunciation of a word or determine or clarify its precise meaning, its part of speech, or its etymology. CCSS.ELA-LITERACY.L.9-10.4.D Verify the preliminary determination of the meaning of a word or phrase (e.g., by checking the inferred meaning in context or in a dictionary). CCSS.ELA-LITERACY.L.9-10.5 Demonstrate understanding of figurative language, word relationships, and nuances in word meanings. CCSS.ELA-LITERACY.L.9-10.5.A Interpret figures of speech (e.g., euphemism, oxymoron) in context and analyze their role in the text. CCSS.ELA-LITERACY.L.9-10.5.B Analyze nuances in the meaning of words with similar denotations. ELD, Part I, B, 6.

<table>
<tr><th>Lesson Routines</th><th>CCSS and ELD Standards Alignment</th></tr>
<tr><td>Step 7:
Collaborative discussion
(TDQ may be answered with a partner or in a small group and/or discussed with whole class)</td><td>CCSS.ELA-LITERACY.SL.9-10.1.A
Come to discussions prepared, having read and researched material under study; explicitly draw on that preparation by referring to evidence from texts and other research on the topic or issue to stimulate a thoughtful, well-reasoned exchange of ideas.

ELD Part I, A.1

ELD Part I, A.3
Offering and justifying opinions, negotiating with and persuading others in communicative exchanges</td></tr>
<tr><td colspan="2">WRITING</td></tr>
<tr><td>Step 8: Text Response</td><td>CCSS.ELA-LITERACY.RL.9-10.2
Determine a theme or central idea of a text and analyze in detail its development over the course of the text, including how it emerges and is shaped and refined by specific details; provide an objective summary of the text.

CCSS.ELA-LITERACY.W.9-10.1
Write arguments to support claims in an analysis of substantive topics or texts, using valid reasoning and relevant and sufficient evidence.

CCSS.ELA-LITERACY.W.9-10.4
Produce clear and coherent writing in which the development, organization, and style are appropriate to task, purpose, and audience.

CCSS.ELA-LITERACY.W.9-10.5
Develop and strengthen writing as needed by planning, revising, editing, rewriting, or trying a new approach, focusing on addressing what is most significant for a specific purpose and audience.

CCSS.ELA-LITERACY.W.9-10.6
Use technology, including the Internet, to produce, publish, and update individual or shared writing products, taking advantage of technology's capacity to link to other information and to display information flexibly and dynamically.

CCSS.ELA-LITERACY.L.9-10.1
Demonstrate command of the conventions of standard English grammar and usage when writing or speaking.

ELD Part I, C 11, 12

ELD Part II
A. Structuring Cohesive Texts, 1. Understanding text structure, 2. Understanding cohesion;
B: Expanding and Enriching Ideas 3. Using verbs and verb phrases 4. Using nouns and noun phrases 5. Modifying to add details;
C. Connecting and condensing ideas, 6. Connecting ideas, 7. Condensing ideas most significant for a specific purpose and audience.

ELD Part I, C, 10

ELD Part II, B 3, 4, 5</td></tr>
<tr><td>Step 9: Self-reflection</td><td>CCSS.ELA-LITERACY.W.9-10.3
Write narratives to develop real or imagined experiences or events using effective technique, well-chosen details, and well-structured event sequences.

CCSS.ELA-LITERACY.W.9-10.3.A
Engage and orient the reader by setting out a problem, situation, or observation, establishing one or multiple point(s) of view, and introducing a narrator and/or characters; create a smooth progression of experiences or events.

CCSS.ELA-LITERACY.W.9-10.3.B
Use narrative techniques, such as dialogue, pacing, description, reflection, and multiple plot lines, to develop experiences, events, and/or characters.</td></tr>
</table>

Lesson Routines	CCSS and ELD Standards Alignment
	CCSS.ELA-LITERACY.W.9-10.3.C Use a variety of techniques to sequence events so that they build on one another to create a coherent whole. CCSS.ELA-LITERACY.W.9-10.3.D Use precise words and phrases, telling details, and sensory language to convey a vivid picture of the experiences, events, setting, and/or characters. CCSS.ELA-LITERACY.W.9-10.3.E Provide a conclusion that follows from and reflects on what is experienced, observed, or resolved over the course of the narrative. CCSS.ELA-LITERACY.W.9-10.4 CCSS.ELA-LITERACY.W.9-10.5
Step 10: Poem writing	CCSS.ELA-LITERACY.W.9-10.6 CCSS.ELA-LITERACY.L.9-10.1 CCSS.ELA-LITERACY.W.9-10.4 CCSS.ELA-LITERACY.W.9-10.5 CCSS.ELA-LITERACY.W.9-10.6 CCSS.ELA-LITERACY.L.9-10.1 ELD Part I, C 10, 12 CCSS.ELA-LITERACY.W.9-10.5 Develop and strengthen writing as needed by planning, revising, editing, rewriting, or trying a new approach, focusing on addressing what is.
Step 11: Prose writing	CCSS.ELA-LITERACY.W.9-10.3 CCSS.ELA-LITERACY.W.9-10.3.A CCSS.ELA-LITERACY.W.9-10.3.B CCSS.ELA-LITERACY.W.9-10.3.C CCSS.ELA-LITERACY.W.9-10.3.D CCSS.ELA-LITERACY.W.9-10.3.E CCSS.ELA-LITERACY.W.9-10.4 CCSS.ELA-LITERACY.W.9-10.5 CCSS.ELA-LITERACY.W.9-10.6 ELD Part II, A 1, 2; B 3, 4, 5; C 6, 7
CULMINATING ACTIVITIES	
Class anthology	CCSS.ELA-LITERACY.W.9-10.4 CCSS.ELA-LITERACY.W.9-10.5 CCSS.ELA-LITERACY.W.9-10.6
Public reading/Presentation	CCSS.ELA-LITERACY.SL.9-10.6 Adapt speech to a variety of contexts and tasks, demonstrating command of formal English when indicated or appropriate. (See grades 9-10 Language standards 1 and 3 here for specific expectations.) ELD Part 1, C, 10

MINDFULNESS PRACTICE SCRIPT FOR STUDENT LEADERS

Roll your shoulders back and down.
Move your head from side to side.
Twist your spine.

Feel your feet on the floor.
Your spine growing taller.
Your hands on your knees.
And your heart to the trees.

Now close your eyes.
Or look down softly.
Relax your forehead and your jaw.
Relax your shoulders.
(Ring bell.)

Notice your breath.
Breathe in. Breathe out. *(3 times)*
Put your hand on your heart and notice how you feel.
Now offer yourself a kind wish. “May you be well and happy.”
(Ring bell.)

About the Author

Laura Bean's teaching career spans three decades. She lived in Kyoto, Japan, for ten years, where she taught ESL and creative writing to university students. Since returning to the United States in 2011, she has been working with English learners and other underserved students in public schools in the San Francisco Bay Area. She earned an MFA in Creative Writing from the University of Arizona and began teaching poetry to young people as a writer-in-residence for Teachers & Writers Collaborative in New York City. She has been practicing mindfulness for three decades, and is a certified Mindful School's Mindful Educator. Her work has been featured in UC Berkeley's *Greater Good Science Center Magazine*, and mostly recently, in an anthology titled *Educating Mindfully: Stories of School Transformation Through Mindfulness*. She is a member of the Coalition of Schools Educating Mindfully. This is her first book. For more information about trainings and writing workshops, visit www.MindfulLiteracy.com.